STORIES OUT OF SCHOOL: MEMORIES AND REFLECTIONS ON CARE AND CRUELTY IN THE CLASSROOM

Contemporary Studies in Social and Policy Issues in Education: The David C. Anchin Center Series

(formerly Social and Policy Issues in Education: The David C. Anchin Center Series)

Kathryn M. Borman, Series Editor

Early Childhood Education: Policy Issues for the 1990s
  edited by Dolores Stegelin, 1992
Contemporary Issues in U.S. Education
  edited by Kathryn M. Borman, Piyushi Swami, and
  Lonnie D. Wagstaff, 1991
Home Schooling: Political, Historical, and Pedagogical Perspectives
  edited by Jan Van Galen and Mary Anne Pitman, 1991
*Effective Schooling for Economically Disadvantaged Students:
School-based Strategies for Diverse Student Populations*
  edited by Howard Johnston and Kathryn M. Borman, 1992
Children Who Challenge the System
  edited by Anne M. Bauer and Ellen M. Lynch, 1993
Minority Education: Anthropological Perspectives
  edited by Evelyn Jacob and Cathie Jordan, 1993
Informing Faculty Development for Teacher Educators
  edited by Kenneth R. Howey and Nancy L. Zimpher, 1994
Investing in U.S. Schools: Directions for Educational Policy
  edited by Bruce A. Jones and Kathryn M. Borman, 1994
Critical Education for Work: Multidisciplinary Approaches
  edited by Richard D. Lakes, 1994

STORIES OUT OF SCHOOL MEMORIES AND REFLECTIONS ON CARE AND CRUELTY IN THE CLASSROOM

edited by
James L. Paul
University of South Florida

and

Terry Jo Smith
National Louis University

Ablex Publishing Corporation
Stamford, Connecticut

Library of Congress Cataloging-in-Publication Data

Stories out of School: memories and reflections on care and cruelty in the class-room / edited by
　　James L. Paul and Terry Jo Smith.
　　　　p.　cm.—(Contemporary studies in social and policy issues in education)
　　Includes bibliographical references and index.
　　ISBN 1-56750-476-0 — ISBN 1-56750-477-9 (pbk.)
　　1.　Critical pedagogy. 2.　Teacher–student relationships. 3.　Classroom environment. I.　Paul, James L. II.　Smith, Terry Jo. III.　Series
　　LC196.S6994　2000
　　370.11'5—dc21
99-36571
CIP

Ablex Publishing Corporation
100 Prospect Street
P.O. Box 811
Stamford, Connecticut 06904-0811

CONTENTS

PREFACE

A lot goes on in a classroom. Many storied accounts of what happens in classrooms have been written, and are being written still. Politicians, parents, and professional educators talk knowingly about students, teachers, curriculum, school, and education. All speak from years of experience and many from the perspective of research and professional preparation. There is no end to the political, social, and moral stories providing accounts of the lived experience of students and teachers.

Educational policy concerns focus on the quality of teaching and the outcomes for students as measured by achievement tests. The higher the test scores, it is argued, the better the teaching. Most research on classrooms has focused on one or some combination of four areas: curriculum; teaching methods; teacher variables such as personality, attitude, skills, and interaction style; and student variables such as intelligence, behavior, socioeconomic status, and learning style.

Educational researchers have attempted to develop valid and reliable measures of these independent variables and to relate them to student achievement. More recently, some researchers have broadened their interest in psychological and social variables to include the moralities and aesthetic qualities of interactions between students and teachers. There is increasing interest in the ethical rules governing relationships and the meaning students make of their experience in the classroom.

While the emphasis of educational policy is on student outcomes in subject areas, there is increasing interest in expanding the means by which those outcomes are achieved. Charter schools, vouchers, and other approaches to school reform are creating instrumental options for educating students. Yet at the same time there is a deregulation of teacher education in order to create more flexible access to the profession in some states.

The reform movement, which many associate with the Carnegie Commission's report on schools in 1983, advanced with the political agenda of securing a stronger competitive economic position in the world. Although there was relatively little input from teachers at that time, teachers have gained more voice and position in the policy debates.

This gain in voice has been accompanied by substantive changes in our understanding of knowledge and the implications of that understanding for the processes of teaching and learning. The shift has been away from an exclusive objectivist view of knowledge, and a narrow behavioral view of learning, to a constructivist understanding of teaching and learning and its implications for the work of teachers and students. Refocusing the lens through which student–teacher interactions are examined has made possible a richer and wider view of experience in the classroom. The aesthetic qualities of the relationships, the affordances of the curriculum, the moralities of teaching, and the meaning of experience can be examined as well as the objective characteristics of students, teachers, and the classroom environment.

The changes in how we understand and study teaching and learning are uneven. Strongly held beliefs support the changes and equally strongly held beliefs challenge them. However, the discourse about teaching and learning and our understandings of the nature of educational research have changed rather dramatically in the last two decades.

These changes form the context for the work described in this book on stories out of school—adult memories of their teachers. The authors have been guided by the work of Jackson (1992), Noddings (1992), Eisner (1998), Palmer (1998), Coles (1989), and Lindley (1993), among others, who have focused on the qualities of life experienced by children, particularly in the classroom. Our interests have centered on memory, meaning, and the self in relationship.

Using a database of letters written by adults (most of whom are teachers or are preparing to be teachers) to their former teachers, we examine the interpersonal spaces shared by teachers and students and the kinds of unacknowledged pedagogies created in those spaces. We are interested in the ethics of experienced pedagogies and the implications of those pedagogies for educating teachers.

In the first chapter we look at story and narrative as a means to construct the teacher–student space. We discuss the impact of feminist scholarship and the work of cultural and critical theorists in the ongoing reenvisioning of teaching and learning. We examine the teacher's power and its impact on the child's construction of self. In this context, we focus on the nature and experience of care and cruelty in the classroom. Our discussion centers on the need to understand the complexity and deep personal meaning of the teacher–student space in restructuring schools into more caring, democratic, and equitable institutions.

In Chapter 2, Paul, Christensen, and Falk describe a method for uncovering hidden stories about teachers and teaching. The method is structured to assist adults in remembering and writing letters (unsent) to teachers who were thoughtful and caring and to those who, by contrast, were cruel and mean-spirited. What has been learned—and is still being learned—from letters containing stories about caring and cruelty in the classroom formed the foundation for this text, and selected letters are found in most of the chapters that follow.

Contrasting images of negative and caring pedagogies are described in Chapters 3 and 4. In Chapter 3, Colucci discusses negative pedagogy, taking us beyond our defenses and repression and begins to name instances of cruelty. In this naming she does not attempt to unearth all cruel educational practices, but provides image after image of negative pedagogy in formal, informal, and hidden curricula. She turns a critical eye to the cruel practices often implicit in school discipline, student evaluation, grouping and tracking, school procedures and rules, instructional practices, and physical plants. In her naming she makes visible many aspects of negative pedagogy that often simply pass as inevitable facts of life, the ways things have always been, or even as sound educational practices. She denaturalizes negative pedagogy by naming it as such, by providing many examples in rapid succession, and by stripping these examples of the contextual norms that camouflage negative practices as institutional necessities.

In Chapter 4, Colucci and Paul discuss caring pedagogy. Caring pedagogy involves all of the positive, consciousness-enhancing life of the classroom orchestrated by a teacher. The predisposition of the teacher to acknowledge, value, and bring into awareness the aesthetic qualities of student performance, of ideas, and of plants, for example, are aspects of a caring pedagogy. The social life of the classroom, the existential centering and growth of self, and the life of the mind are deeply connected. The experience of caring and being cared for provides the deep continuity of what children come to know and how they come to know it. Colucci and Paul examine caring pedagogy from the perspective of developing the capacity to care as well as enhancing the quality of learning about self and others.

In Chapter 5, Martinez and Smith construct the shared relational space between teachers and students through the storied lens of culture and history. They examine ways schools have functioned historically as mechanisms of cultural imperialism. Cultural differences have been viewed as educational handicaps, or worse, as indicative of inferior intelligence, moral fiber, and life experiences. Schools' historical efforts to eliminate differences have been played out in individual relationships within school contexts. Many of the people who wrote letters to hurtful teachers spoke of being humiliated and denigrated by teachers on the basis of race, gender, or social class. Martinez and Smith construct these relationships within a greater institutional and social/political history of schooling, allowing us to see in essence how the "pain within us reflects the structures outside of us."

In Chapter 6, Houck focuses on the ethical dimension of school life and the complexity of ethical choices made by teachers. She examines ethical deliberation within the context of pedagogy. Building on the premise that teachers have a great deal of power and influence in relationships with students, Houck looks at the complex issues involved in making educational decisions. She reflects on perspectives that influence our views of what "ought" to be done and suggests a focus on relationships as essential in ethical deliberation about "right and wrong" behaviors.

In Chapter 7, Smith and Perez examine powerful spaces between teachers and students through the stories of teachers who have authored texts of their experiences within schools. These teachers' stories show that the spaces shared with students are powerful spaces for them as well as for their students. Sylvia Ashton Warner's "School Teacher" is a classic text filled with the emotion of caring for students' growth at a deep spiritual level. Lou Anne Johnson's "Girls in the Back of the Room" is a more contemporary story with many similar themes. Power is a theme in these stories that goes two ways. In these teacher's stories we see the constant tension between meeting the institutional needs of the system, fitting into its rhetoric and mores, and meeting the unique human needs of their students. In these stories we see teachers beginning to take a deep personal authorship of their own experiences within schools. We see them grappling with the power of the educational institutions that form a context for their relationships with students, and becoming empowered to reconstruct their relationships with students in more caring and affirming ways.

In Chapter 8, Smith and Danforth focus on teachers' journeys into their own disowned pasts. It includes the writing of several teachers who bravely look into their own histories to confront the racist, sexist, classist, and ablist attitudes that they have generated toward others. In this chapter we see reflective teaching taken to a very deep level. These teachers' stories represent courageous attempts to stop assigning blame to other peoples' prejudice and cruel practices and instead turn the light inward, illuminating ways in which they have harmed others. The purpose of this reflection is not a confession of sins in an attempt to absolve themselves of guilt, but an attempt to take conscious responsibility for their unintended actions.

Born into a society that is riddled with racism, sexism, classism, and ablism, it would be virtually impossible not to have internalized some of these hurtful ways of seeing others. However, as long as we demonize these aspects of our histories and cultures and distance ourselves from them, as long as we can only see them in others but not in ourselves, we continue to hurt the children we are entrusted to educate.

REFERENCES

Coles, R. (1989). *The call of stories: Teaching and the moral imagination.* Boston: Houghton Mifflin.

Eisner, E. (1998). *The enlightened eye: Qualitative inquiry and the enhancement of educational practice.* Columbus, OH: Merrill.

Jackson, P. (1992). *Untaught lessons.* New York: Teachers College Press.

Lindley, D. A. (1993). *This rough magic: The life of teaching.* Westport, CT: Bergen & Garvey.

Noddings, N. (1992). *The challenge to care in schools: An alternative approach to education.* New York: Teachers College Press.

Palmer, P. (1998) *The courage to teach: Exploring the inner landscape of a teacher's life.* San Francisco: Jossey-Bass.

SHARING SPACE, NEGOTIATING POWER, AND CREATING MEANING IN THE CLASSROOM

Terry Jo Smith
National-Louis University

James L. Paul
University of South Florida

These are the teachers who are remembered years afterward; not necessarily with love, but at least with awe mixed with some measure of affection. They are remembered because they have done something somewhere within the student's psyche. My hypothesis is that they have successfully touched what Lopez-Pedraza calls an "afflicted spot." Where the student felt pain, puzzlement, frustration—a deep unknowing, too deep to be acknowledged—the teacher brought healing. Order, method, and peace were substituted for chaos and uncertainty and hurt. How does this happen?

For one thing, I believe such teachers have never lost sight of what they received from their teachers. They have remained full of gratitude for the healing they received. I do not believe anyone can successfully teach who has not been successfully taught. . . . Lineage is a key to good teaching: How we teach is not just made up on the spot.
(Lindley, 1993, p. 120)

SACRED PLACES

A few years ago, the first author of this chapter was teaching an undergraduate education class and the subject of discussion turned to the nature of teacher–student relationships. The question these preservice teachers were pondering had to do with negotiating the space between teacher and students. How close do you allow yourself to get to your students? What is the correct "professional distance" a teacher should maintain? How involved should a teacher become in a student's personal life? How much of a teacher's self should be disclosed? How and where do teachers construct boundaries between students and self?

A young man stated that he believed we needed to limit our roles with students to those directly involved with teaching. He spoke of liability, of not being able to save the world, of the emotional toll on teachers of getting too involved. He was convincing and much of what he said resonated with many of the students' experiences with their own teachers past and present. A few other students spoke up in support of his position, citing the need to focus on the teacher's primary task of teaching the three Rs and the risks of getting too involved beyond this role.

A young woman near the back of the room raised her hand and asked to speak. She stood up, although this was not a custom in this class, and leaned heavily on the desk in front of her for support. Her chest heaved in and out as she seemed to be gathering the courage to speak. Finally, as tears ran down her face, she began to tell her story in a voice choked with emotion.

> When I was 16 my mother left our family. It came as a total surprise and me and my brothers and sisters were devastated. I felt so ashamed. So lost. My father was dealing with his own loss. My mother was our connection; without her we all just withdrew into our own sadness and fear. I couldn't even think about going to school so I just stopped going. Up until then I was a good student, but I felt so sad and so ashamed I didn't think I could face my friends or care about what was in a book. After a few weeks my journalism teacher called me and asked why I hadn't been in school. I told her we were having some family problems and I didn't think I could come back. She spoke to me of the importance of an education and the promise I'd shown as a student. But I felt so unable to face school or life for that matter.
>
> Two days later this teacher showed up at my house. She was the only person in the world who seemed to care about what was happening to me at that terrible time in my life. I told her what happened with my mother. We talked for over two hours and she convinced me to come back to school. From that time on she took a special interest in me. When I had problems I talked to her about them. I talked to her about boys and my sisters and brothers. I asked her questions my mother used to answer for me.
>
> I am standing here today because a teacher took a chance and got involved. I don't know where I would be if she didn't. If I can give that back to a child, I'm gonna do it.

When she stopped speaking, the class sat quietly for what seemed like a long time. There were few dry eyes. There was nothing like this in their textbooks. The responsibility and the possibilities of their future professions had just taken on new dimensions as this brave young woman shared her heart and her journey. She had not forgotten the deep personal healing that had taken place in her own life in relationship to a very caring teacher and it was these lessons of the heart that guided her thinking about how she would approach relationships with her own students some day.

A few weeks later, I was in one of my own doctoral classes in which the second author of this chapter introduced the letter-writing activity that has provided an integrative focus for this text. (The rationale and procedures used for the letter-writing process are described in Chapter 3.) Danforth, another doctoral student, read a letter he had written (but had not intended to send) to a coach who had hurt his feelings when he was a child. In response, each of the students in my cohort was asked to write a similar letter to a teacher in our pasts who we felt had hurt us. After writing, we were invited to read the letters to the group if we wanted to.

There was one woman in our group who was rather shy. I was surprised when she offered to read the letter she wrote to a teacher she had in a junior high school science class. As she read her letter to a man who had humiliated her on several occasions in front of the class, she started to cry and then to sob. The man had made fun of her Irish heritage, chided her for distracting the boys in the class, and insinuated that she had a bad reputation. Twenty-five years had not healed the deep hurt experienced at the hands of a cruel teacher. As I watched my friend voice her long-buried pain, I realized that teachers have a tremendous amount of power.

In conducting the research for this book, we asked many people to journey into these more sacred dimensions of learning. We have asked them to remember both hurt and healing and to confront, in their imaginations, the teachers who touched their psyches for good and for harm. What has been unearthed in these many personal journeys are places of powerful emotion, often long ago buried, but not resolved. In the act of remembering these more personal aspects of education, we reenter the shared spaces between teacher and student, spaces that transcend the learning of facts and figures, to learning of self worth, and what Thomas Moore called "soulful learning."

SHARING SPACES OF UNEQUAL POWER

Lindley (1993) describes teaching that "begins not with knowledge, but with personal reflection begun in the teacher and continued in the student; its goal is equality of teacher and student, an equality conferred by occupying shared imaginal space" (p. 60). Teachers enter this "shared imaginal space" with more power than students. As adults they naturally have more experience and "knowledge" than students do. As teachers they naturally occupy a position of more power in school. This unequal power relationship contributes to the teacher's potential to do both great good and great harm. Noblit (1993) offers the following portrait of a powerful teacher's power as witnessed in the ritual of hand-raising and participation in a group lesson.

> Repeatedly, children would simply look at their classmates with smiles on their faces after being called upon, whether or not they offered an answer. It was their moment in the sun.
>
> Pam (the teacher), of course, was the brightest sun even though the children would also look to each other for recognition. When Pam called on you, it was as if you were the chosen, and it seemed to matter little that others would be chosen and that your moment was but brief. How did a public testing become a moment in the sun? In a multitude of small things. In calling on the children, Pam would let the hands wave for a while—long enough to allow the maximum number of hands to raise. In this time, she would smile and make eye contact with all she could. She raised the event to a fever pitch and then chose. After the choice, her attention was focused on the chosen child. (p. 33)

The power of this teacher is almost scary. The very act of bestowing her attention on students seems to bolster their self-confidence and status among their classmates. When this power is wielded in caring ways it can be part of a healing and growing process. A teacher's position as authority and leader in the classroom magnifies the importance of her actions, attitudes, and words in students' lives. Young children often assume teachers are all-knowing and all-powerful adults, much like their parents. What a teacher seems to "know" about a child takes on great significance. Children who see their own worth reflected in a teacher's eyes, words, and actions can confidently enter into learning and comfortably fit into a classroom. They can move easily into those vulnerable places of learning. When they feel affirmed as human beings, children can take chances, explore, and venture into new territories.

The impact of teachers' power that is not used in loving and affirming ways can wound a child in ways that may never completely heal. Alice Miller (1990a, 1990b, 1997) has written convincingly of the catastrophic effects of being punished, rejected, and rigidly controlled as children. She believes that the ill treatment of children by parents and teachers is the root of violence in our society. Miller (1990b) writes:

> A person who can understand and integrate his anger as part of himself will not become violent. He has the need to strike out at others only if he is thoroughly unable to understand his rage, if he was not permitted to become familiar with this feeling as a small child, was never able to experience it as part of himself because such a thing was totally unthinkable in his surroundings. (p. 65)

Rather than recognize the cruelty suffered at the hands of these "authority" figures, children accept the pain and cruelty meted out to them as actions both deserved by them and "for their own good." Later in life, they often heap the same abuses on their own children or students in the name of necessary discipline rather than confront the pain of their own upbringing and education. Miller (1990b) writes:

> For children who have grown up being assailed for qualities the parents hate in themselves can hardly wait to assign these qualities to someone else so they can once again regard themselves as good, "moral," noble, and altruistic. Such projections can easily become part of any Weltanschauung (worldview).
>
> The pedagogical conviction that one must bring a child into line from the outset has its origin in the need to split off the disquieting parts of the inner self and project them onto an available object. The child's great plasticity, flexibility, defenselessness, and availability make it the ideal object for this projection. The enemy within can at last be hunted down on the outside. (p. 11)

The incredible power evident in Noblit's description of Pam, the second-grade teacher, can be used in life-affirming or life-denying ways. The impact of this power in the child's construction of self and the attributes assigned to self may last far into his or her future. The way power is experienced in one's childhood impacts greatly how one interacts with and uses power as an adult. This, then, has implications for how we might understand teachers' actions in relationship to their students and in relationship to others in the school systems in which they work. In exploring the complexity of teacher–student relationships within schools we must also understand that teachers share relationships with administrators in which they are in the vulnerable position of having less power. Their own histories in relationship to those in authority are often echoed in their adult life in relationship to those with more power.

> If an adult has not developed a mind of his own, then he will find himself at the mercy of the authorities for better or worse, just as an infant finds itself at the mercy of its parents. Saying no to those more powerful will always seem too threatening to him. (Miller, 1990b, p. 84)

When the relational spaces between individuals within schools are structured in terms of dominance/subordination, those involved may play both roles simultaneously. The tragic replaying of abuse by those who have been abused themselves is a familiar yet perplexing phenomenon. Teachers who interact within the system through an underlying dynamic of obedience, will necessarily demand obedience of their own students. That is part of what is required from the authorities. If they are unable to question the dictates of the system, they will not be able to allow their students to question the dictates in their classrooms. They do not so much try to control their students of their own volition, but out of a deference for authority.

In a sense, this allows them to absolve themselves of personal responsibility and guilt. If the decision is not theirs to make, then they are not responsible for their part in the diffuse web of power and control. Miller (1990b) writes:

> Our whole system of raising and educating children provides the power-hungry with a ready-made railway network they can use to reach the destination of their choice. They need only push the buttons that parents and educators have already installed. (p. 20)

In the two examples of teachers' power given at the beginning of this chapter, we see extreme examples of teacher power in action. In one case a teacher uses her power to care for a young girl who struggles with her mother's abandonment. The teacher in some ways fills the empty space the mother has left and provides the child with the support she needs to face her friends, in spite of deep sadness and shame, and finish high school. She even inspires her to become a teacher herself—a teacher who understands the tremendous potential for healing that her role could entail. In the story of the abusive teacher described above, we see the opposite side of the coin. Here a teacher uses his position of authority literally to commit crimes against a child. These are extreme cases in some ways, but not in others. They resonate within us with stories of our own.

SEEING AND BELIEVING

> Power-over works like sorcery: it casts a spell on us. It changes our consciousness, clouds our vision so that we don't notice it in operation. (Starhawk, 1987, p. 95)

Much of teacher education has focused on methods of instruction, assessment, and classroom management. This focus on method has historical roots in modernist philosophies of science in which method has been given a place of prominence that historically has obscured and negated aspects of teaching and learning that are not "observable" (Beyer, 1992; Noddings, 1991). By focusing on observable and measurable behaviors, we effectively have evaded deep critical reflection on the more complex issues of power in education.

In recent years, however, there has been an influx of counter discourses that have begun to "bring into a place of constructed visibility" (Lather, 1994) the issues of power that are implicit in our educational practices. These educators have begun to move out of the lines imposed by the rigid requirements of traditional research into interpretive ways of knowing that construct textured narratives of educational contexts through engagement in those contexts. Critical and cultural theorists (Giroux, 1988, 1991; McLaren, 1991, 1994) have begun to look at how education actually works at a broad cultural level to maintain the status quo and sort students along the lines of social class and race. Feminist theorists are beginning to open up dialogues about power in schools (Gilligan, 1982; Kelly, 1997). Teachers, as researchers, are beginning to tell stories about their own contexts which unearth the issues of power that have long been repressed (Cochran-Smith & Lytle, 1993; Gitlin & Russell, 1994; Neumann & Peterson, 1997). Proponents of such philosophies as "whole language" are reenvisioning the learning process as a dialogical endeavor, rather than a passive act of learning language and "authority." All of these changes and challenges to power echo those occurring in other disciplines and other sectors of society.

Changes in how we see and structure power in education have very personal implications for each of us. Attempts to restructure education, to empower teachers and students, and to make schools into more democratic institutions have met with considerable resistance (Cuban, 1993). In light of Miller's theories, this resistance makes much sense. The structuring of power in relationships is deeply rooted in our own histories. Attempts to change education that treat it as something separate and outside of those who comprise it have failed because the structures that we have grown up within—family, community, and school—also structure our own experiences of self and other. Starhawk (1987) sums this up succinctly: "The pain within us is a mirror of the power structures outside us" (p. 7).

When we attempt to restructure education, we cannot be uninvolved spectators. We must also be willing to confront our own histories even when it means confronting our own pain within. In remembering our positions as students, we can get back in touch with the power-full effects of schooling on our self-images and self-esteem. When we look back and construct stories of the painful aspects of our pasts we can begin to break down the wall of silence that keeps the painful process of cruelty circling through generations. By the same token, stories of teachers who have shared power with us in loving and equitable ways allow us to connect to our own growth and healing. This lineage, Lindly tells us, is the key to becoming a good teacher. We are not just made on the spot.

CARE AND CARING IN THE CLASSROOM

While Alice Miller, a psychoanalyst, has helped us understand the nature of cruelty and its effects on children, Nel Noddings, an educator, has helped us understand the nature of caring and the urgent need to care for children in schools. She sees the lack of emphasis on care and caring to be one of the most serious challenges in our culture. Both the need to be cared for and the need to care for others are largely unmet. This is especially true in schools.

She describes the difficulties of those who appear not to care, those who experience themselves as uncared for, and those who act on a socially destructive understanding of care. Recognizing the complexity of care and caring in relationships, she seeks a balanced understanding of the positive force of care in human communities, including the classroom. Noddings includes ideas, animals, plants, and causes as well as people in her view of care.

In schools, the emphasis on academic knowledge and skills has so overshadowed our concern for the qualities of relationships that we do not give much attention to relational issues in the selection of teachers, the evaluation of teaching, or teacher preparation. The high priority placed on outcome accountability tends to silence concern with the interpersonal processes and classroom cultures that produce the objectively measurable outcomes. Noddings argues that the academic goals cannot be achieved without providing caring and continuity for students.

She challenges the single-mindedness of the focus on intellectual development to the exclusion of the broader social, emotional, and spiritual needs of children. Writing as an educational philosopher, a former math teacher, and a mother, Noddings points out that the more humanistic and caring approach to teaching does not necessarily reduce the importance of math and science in the curriculum. She writes:

> Classrooms should be places in which students can legitimately act on a rich variety of purposes, in which wonder and curiosity are alive, in which dedication to full human growth. . . . will not stunt or impede intellectual achievement, but even if it might, I would take the risk if I could produce people who would live nonviolently with each other, sensitively and in harmony with the natural environment, reflectively and serenely with themselves. (1992, p. 12)

Ethicists, including Noddings, have cautioned policy makers about the shortsightedness of ends, however laudable, justifying the means. There is no limit to the nefarious instrumental possibilities for teachers to produce gain scores in math and science. The balanced view Noddings advocates suggests that our "bottom line" thinking about achievement-based accountability forces a false choice. Following strongly in the tradition of John Dewey, Noddings observes that the child's experience and what he or she learns are inseparable. The social formation and moral development of children embedded in the processes of education, then, are at least as important as the development of knowledge and skills in science and mathematics.

Noddings's definition of care follows on Heidegger's view that care is "the very Being of human life" (1992, p. 15), the ultimate reality of life. She characterizes a caring relation as "a connection or encounter between two human beings—a carer and a recipient of care, or cared-for" (p. 15). In this relational view of caring, Noddings points out that a student must receive care in order for caring to occur. A teacher's efforts in caring are not sufficient; the student must know herself to be cared for.

In her earlier work, *Caring, A Feminine Approach to Ethics and Moral Education,* Noddings described caring as engrossment and motivational displacement, a state of consciousness in which there is an "open, nonselective receptivity to the cared-for" (p. 15). Similar to Simone Weil's view of attention as the center of love for neighbor, Noddings described engrossment as "an emptying of the soul of all its own contents in order to receive the other" (p. 16).

> When I care, I really hear, see, or feel what the other tries to convey. The engrossment or attention may last only a few moments and it may or may not be repeated in future encounters, but it is full and essential in any caring encounter. (p. 16)

Noddings' view of engrossment is similar to what Barbara McClintock, who won the Nobel Prize in 1983 for her work in genetics, saw as a deep relationship between a scientist and what she sought to study. Evelyn Fox Keller, writing McClintock's biography, comments, "Over and over again she tells us one must have the time to look, the patience to 'hear what the material has to say to you,' the openness to 'let it come to you'" (qtd. in Palmer, 1998, p. 55).

For Noddings, caring is relational, not an individual virtue. She does, however, recognize the varying capacities of individuals, including teachers and students, to enter into caring relations. Teachers, she argues, "not only have to create caring relations in which they are the carers, but that they also have a responsibility to help their students develop the capacity to care" (1992, p. 18).

Children need support in gaining awareness of and learning how to value themselves, others, plants, animals, and ideas, for example, in thoughtful ways. Such awareness comes with nurture and thoughtfulness in helping children and youth with the questions they raise about themselves such as "Who am I? What kind of person will I be? Who will love me? How do others see me?" (Noddings, 1992, p. 20). Noddings charges that "schools spend more time on the quadratic formula than on any of these existential questions" (p. 20).

Noddings goes beyond Dewey's emphasis on forging a relation between a child's experience and subject matter to argue that "There are few things that all students need to know, and it ought to be acceptable for students to reject some material in order to pursue other topics with enthusiasm. Caring teachers listen and respond differentially to their students" (1992, p. 19). Speaking to a similar deep understanding of interpersonal relationships, Keller characterized McClintock's genius for knowing as "love that allows for intimacy without the annihilation of difference" (qtd. in Palmer, 1998, p. 55).

Care and caring implicate ethical considerations. Noddings (1984) argues that an ethic of care is an ethic of relation, not an ethic of virtue. It recognizes the responsibility of the individual to develop the capacity to care and to be cared for. She suggests that moral education, viewed in the context of an ethic of care, has four components: modeling, dialogue, practice, and confirmation (1984). Modeling is essential because the point is to show how to care for others in our relationships with them; it is not an abstract principle to be taught. Modeling and caring occur simultaneously. Caring is the moral orientation that gives meaning to our behavior and justifies our decisions as a model.

Dialogue, the second component, is "a common search for understanding, empathy, or appreciation. It can be playful or serious, logical or imaginative, goal or process oriented, but is always a genuine quest for something undetermined at the beginning" (Noddings, 1992, p. 23). It is implied in the criterion of engrossment. Dialogue helps inform moral choices and it provides a connection between the one making a decision and the one(s) about whom a decision is being made. It proceeds from the assumption that we are best at making caring choices when we understand the needs and the history of the needs of others.

Practice, the third component, relates to the attitudes and mentalities shaped by experience. Our institutions and training programs promote attitudes and worldviews as well as provide specific programs to develop skills. If we intend for people to have a positive care orientation in their moral constructions of the world, then we must provide opportunities for them to experience and develop skills in caring and being cared for. Noddings sees the practice of a care-based moral education as having the potential to transform schools. She also cautions that care, misunderstood, could be incorporated into the daily routines and business-as-usual life of the school and become meaningless.

Confirmation, the fourth component, involves affirming and encouraging the best in others. It is grounded in trust and "lifts us toward our vision of a better self" (Noddings, 1992, p. 25). Unlike some religious perspectives, confirmation here is meant to keep the person in connection with the one about whom a decision is being made rather than standing apart and judging the person. It recognizes in the other his or her own moral struggle, or potential to struggle.

CONSTRUCTING MEMORIES AND FUTURES:
AN INTRODUCTION TO THE STORIES IN THIS TEXT

Patti Lather (1994) speaks of critical research as a means of bringing power relationships into a space of constructed visibility. In this book, we attempt to make visible the power-full relationships that occur in schools in the space between teachers and students. Rather than try to access this space through observation and measurement, we address it through memory in the form of letters written to teachers who have been helpful, or hurtful, and through reflection on school practices. In these reflections, we see not only our stories, but echoes of the social structures in which our lives have been situated. It is not surprising that stories of racism, sexism, classism, and ablism emerge when we begin to tell our stories of teacher–student relationships. These are the same stories we find when we look at the broader social history of educational practice (Giroux, 1988, 1991; McLaren, 1991, 1994).

Iris Young (1990), heavily influenced by the work of Julia Kristeva, tells us that racism (and the other hurtful "-isms" that plague our society) is often acted out within our relationships and experienced as a feeling of aversion for different groups of people. Since it is no longer socially acceptable to assert racist beliefs openly, racism has gone underground and is deeply embedded in unconscious and unintended acts. In order to change the social and educational structures that sustain and perpetuate oppressive and cruel treatment, we must look into our own feelings of aversion toward various groups.

> Power-over is maintained by the belief that some people are more valuable than others. Its systems reflect distinctions in value. When we refuse to accept those distinctions, refuse to automatically assume our powerlessness, the smooth functioning of the systems of oppression is interrupted. Each interruption creates a small space, a rip in the fabric of oppression that has the potential to let another power come through. (Starhawk, 1987, p. 84)

In the act of telling our stories, we make dimensions of schooling visible which have long been obscured in our focus on methods rather than meanings. However, the stories we tell are our creations and this gives us meaningful ways to reflect on the selves and positionings of the selves that create the stories. Narrative, with its ability to delve into how education is experienced in body and soul, allows us to access social, political, and ethical dimensions of schooling which are often "controlled out" of our educational research.

In a sense, we must look into our own educational histories to create new futures. When we begin to bring the powerful spaces between students and teachers into a place of constructed visibility, we can begin to construct those spaces in more caring and ethical ways. It is this space and its construction that is the concern of this book. We intend to inquire into school relationships and construct them from many positions in the hope of creating a tapestry of meaning, a composite of many threads of experience of those vulnerable and powerful spaces of teacher–student relationships.

Teachers go into teaching with high ideals and good intentions. Most go about their work caring for children, unacclaimed except in the cherished memories of their students. On the other hand, many, perhaps more than our folklore about teachers and teaching acknowledge, are cruel.

The cruel teachers you read about in the letters presented throughout this book are not people who are inherently evil, who wake up in the morning with the mission of hurting or humiliating children throughout the school day. They are most likely individuals who believe that what they do is for students' own good, or a necessary by-product of maintaining the order of the system. Often these teachers believe they are responding to something evil in the child, something which they need to stamp out, unaware that what they are seeing in the child is as much a product of their own histories, experiences, social position, teacher training, and prejudice as it is a part of the child. The most cruel actions of teachers may be directed at those children who remind the teacher of what she values least, and, perhaps has least acknowledged, in herself.

If we are going to restructure education into a more caring, democratic, and equitable endeavor, we must begin to focus on the vulnerable and powerful spaces of school relationships. If we can begin to bring into conscious awareness the ways in which the pain inside of us reflects the structures outside, we can begin to transform education and society into more charitable and inclusive spaces. If we are willing to look into our own histories and embrace the love and comfort as well as the pain and cruelty which have deeply impacted our means of interacting with others, we can begin to purposefully construct schools in ways that nourish the development of healthy children—mind, heart, body, and soul.

REFERENCES

Beyer, L. E. (1992). The personal and the social in education. In E. W. Ross, J. Cornett, & G. McCutcheon (Eds.), *Teacher personal theorizing: Connecting curriculum, practice, theory, and research* (pp. 239–256). Albany: State University of New York Press.

Cochran-Smith, M., & Lytle, S. (1993). *Inside/outside: Teacher research and knowledge.* New York: Teachers College Press.

Cuban, L. (1993). *How teachers taught: Constancy and change in American classrooms* (2nd ed.). New York: Teachers College Press.

Gilligan, C. (1982). *In a different voice.* Cambridge: Harvard University Press.

Giroux, H. A. (1988). *Teachers as intellectuals: Toward a critical pedagogy of learning.* New York: Bergin and Garvey.

Giroux, H. A. (1991). Postmodernism as border pedagogy: Redefining the boundaries of race and ethnicity. In H. A. Giroux (Ed.), *Postmodernism, feminism, and cultural politics: Redrawing educational boundaries* (pp. 217–256). Albany: State University of New York Press.

Gitlin, A., & Russell, R. (1994). Alternative methodologies and the research context. In A. Gitlin (Ed.), *Power and method* (pp. 181–202). New York: Routledge.

Kelly, U. A. (1997). *Schooling desire: Literacy, cultural politics, and pedagogy.* New York: Routledge.

Lather, P. (1994). Fertile obsession: Validity after poststructuralism. In A. Gitlin (Ed.), *Power and Method* (pp. 36–60). New York: Routledge.

Lindley, D. A. (1993). *This rough magic: The life of teaching.* Westport, CT: Bergen & Garvey.

McLaren, P. (1991). Schooling the postmodern body: Critical pedagogy and the politics of enfleshment. In H. A. Giroux (Ed.), *Postmodernism, feminisim, and cultural politics: Redrawing educational boundaries* (pp. 144–173). Albany: State University of New York Press.

McLaren, P. (1994). Multiculturalism and the postmodern critique: Toward a pedagogy of resistance and transformation. In H. A. Giroux & P. McLaren (Eds.), *Between borders: Pedagogy and the politics of cultural studies* (192–219). New York: Routledge.

Miller, A. (1990a). *For your own good: Hidden cruelty in child-rearing and the roots of violence.* New York: The Noonday Press.

Miller, A. (1990b). *Thou shalt not be aware: Society's betrayal of the child* (3rd ed.). New York: Meridian.

Miller, A. (1997). *Breaking down the wall of silence: The liberating experince of facing painful truth.* New York: Meridian.

Neuman, A., & Peterson, P. (1997). *Learning from our lives: Woman, research and autobiography in education.* New York: Teachers College Press.

Noblit, G. (1993) Power and caring. *American Educational Research Journal, 30*(1), 23–38.

Noddings, N. (1984). *Caring: A feminist approach to ethics and moral education.* Berkeley: University of California Press.

Noddings, N. (1991). Stories in dialogue: Caring and interpersonal relationships. In C. Witherell & N. Noddings (Eds.), *Stories lives tell: Narrative and dialogue in education* (pp. 157–170). New York: Teachers College Press.

Noddings, N. (1992). *The challenge to care in schools.* New York: Teachers College Press.

Palmer, P. (1998). *The courage to teach: Exploring the inner landscape of a teacher's life.* San Francisco: Jossey-Bass.

Starhawk. (1987). *Truth or dare: Encounters with power, authority, and mystery.* San Francisco: Harper.

Young, I. M. (1990). *Justice and the politics of difference.* Princeton: Princeton University Press.

2

ACCESSING THE INTIMATE SPACES OF LIFE IN THE CLASSROOM THROUGH LETTERS TO FORMER TEACHERS: A PROTOCOL FOR UNCOVERING HIDDEN STORIES

James L. Paul
University of South Florida

Linda Christensen
Montana State University

George Falk
Cornerstone Christian School, Saskatchewan

Writing of a memory is a process of gaining access to interior life, a kind of literary archeology: on the basis of some information and a little guesswork you journey to a site to see what remains were left behind and to reconstruct the world that these remains imply.
(Morrison, 1987, p. 106)

> It is our inward journey that leads us through time—forward or back, seldom in a straight line, most often spiraling. Each of us is moving, changing, with respect to others. As we discover, we remember, remembering, we discover; and most intensely do we experience this when our separate journeys converge. Our living experience at those meeting points is one of the charged dramatic fields of fiction.
>
> (Welty, 1984, p. 102)

In 1990, the first author of this chapter agreed to speak to a group of teachers about affect in the classroom. It was a familiar topic to me, and I knew what was generally expected in the presentation. However, I had never been very satisfied with our approaches to thinking and talking about how affect is manifested in the classroom and in its role in learning. Research had not been very helpful in describing the role of the emotional lives of students in their learning. Neither had it helped us understand how the emotional lives of teachers impacted their students.

In my own experience, I knew that teachers had helped shape the way I thought about others, my values, and my feelings about myself as a learner. Some of the influences were positive and some were not. I remember teachers who I believe genuinely cared about me. There were others who, in retrospect, probably should not have been in the classroom. As a teacher educator I knew our curriculum in the professional preparation of teachers did not address this issue in any serious way. The emotional life of the student preparing to be a teacher is not a focus in teacher education; yet we know that teachers share spaces with students in which they function as architects of meaning construction and models in the exercise of power. Fortunately, during the past decade, several educators have focused a great deal of attention on teachers' power and their constructive influence on the curriculum and the lives of students (Jackson, 1992; Noblit, 1993; Noddings, 1991).

I went to the presentation with a plan to help these teachers remember their own teachers. I was interested in their affective memories and the ways those memories influenced their own behavior and attitudes in the classroom. I divided the session into two parts: memories of teachers who are remembered as caring and those who are remembered as cruel or mean spirited. I used a letter-writing protocol and guided the teachers in remembering their former teachers and writing letters to them. The letters were not intended to be sent but to be used for purposes of their own learning.

This process of remembering and writing has been refined over the past eight years and we have worked with many teachers using the letter-writing protocol. Many of them have been willing to share their letters with us to help us learn more about the power that teachers have and how that power is passed on to their students who, themselves, become teachers.

In this chapter we describe the perspective guiding our work and then discuss the method we have used with students in teacher education programs and in in-service programs to help them examine their own life experiences in school and how those experiences might impact their teaching.

PERSPECTIVE

Discovering "Self" Through Stories

A growing approach to examining our ways of being and knowing is to examine the stories of our past (Diamond, 1993; Kelchtermans, 1993; Witherell & Noddings, 1991). Our lives are made up of stories, some told over and over, fond memories that we tell and retell, fashioning them anew with rich or fading memories. Others are hidden in our unconscious, waiting to be uncovered, triggered alive by a chance meeting, an evocative aroma, a visit to a remembered place. Embedded in all of these stories of our lives are the seeds and the structures of our selves, the foundations and walls of our beings, why we are the way we are. Our stories reveal the "thickness of our personal identity" (Brockelman, 1985) and, as Witherell (1991) says, our sense of our lives is embedded in what we make and remake of what happens to us.

The formulation of the self involves two major processes. One is social formation, involving the ways we define and are defined by our social and cultural contexts. The other involves our relationships—our sense of self in affiliation with others and the meaning systems that evolve from our mutual experiences. Together, these processes provide a framework for our daily lives in the ways that we learn, in what we perceive, in what we value, and in how we relate to each other (Grumet, 1991).

Stories of our experiences that we remember are self-defining moments in our life. In the remembering we recreate the event as we saw it, felt it, as it impacted us. In that remembering we change the event, but we are telling about what it meant to us personally. Stories help us make the abstract concrete and accessible; they impose order and coherence on the stream of experience so we can work out the meanings of events in our past.

Ways of Knowing Through Narrative

Through personal experience, people make sense of the world and the reservoir of these experiences is one source of teachers' theories of practice (McCutcheon, 1992). Our experiences are shared in stories. A story is a theory of something; what we tell and how we tell it reveals what we believe (Carter, 1993). Stories help us understand our experiences and in them we wander into insights (Diamond, 1993).

McCutcheon (1992) has suggested three reasons for bringing our stories into conscious awareness. The first is to examine and reconstruct, if necessary, our past experiences in order to understand them. Second is to bring into consciousness aspects of ourselves of which we may not have been aware. Third is to create more self-confidence by gaining knowledge and control of more aspects of ourselves.

The Role and Power of Narrative in Education

One of the least developed areas of teacher education programs is helping students take a look at how their "self" enters into what they will be as teachers. This is also true of in-service teacher education programs. We have teachers write their philosophies of education or why they want to be a teacher, but we have not really had them examine who they are, what their personal beliefs and values are, and what it is within them that will guide how they will teach. The frozen seas of the self are an important but neglected part of teacher education (Diamond, 1993).

There is wisdom in the adage "you will teach as you were taught." All aspects of past education and training are reflected in the construction of learning and how learning is directed or facilitated. Indeed, the very reasons for choosing to be a teacher can be found in the self of the teacher (Hargreaves & Tucker, 1991). Beyond that, teachers' professional behaviors are largely determined by and understood from their experiences.

One way of having students reflect on these ideas would be to have them describe events from their years in school and to weave those stories into a picture of themselves as a person being or becoming a teacher. This process of reflective reconstruction is what Dewey (1916) referred to as the essential definition of education itself. He concluded that education is "that reconstruction or reorganization of experience which adds to the meaning of experience, and which increases ability to direct the course of subsequent experience" (p. 76).

We are uncovering the traces left by childhood and examining how our experiences impact on adult orientations and conceptions of teaching. Storytelling enables us to re-live, in a sense, things lost in the unconscious, yet not quite forgotten. It engages us personally and provides a wonderful starting point for students in education to begin their formal teacher preparation reflectively, enabling them to connect to past with their future and become aware of the becoming part of their education (Weber, 1993).

Teachers can also use stories to learn a lesson about the construction of relationships between teacher and student in a particular time in a classroom. The stories we tell about teachers and events that happened to us in school contain images of care, of relationships with important people in our lives. Indeed, as Witherell (1991) says, our self is formed and given meaning in the context of our relations with others. Noddings (1991), in discussing the importance of reflecting on care in the classroom, says being cared for is a prerequisite for learning to care.

PROTOCOL FOR UNCOVERING STORIES

Letter Writing Activity

Teacher educators may want to include some activities in their courses that help their students look at past experiences in their lives that may have influenced their decision to become a teacher and their beliefs about teaching. Following is the process that we have developed to stimulate such an examination of life stories. The process involves asking students to remember teachers that they have had in the past, and especially teachers who had an impact on their lives. The students then write letters to these teachers, relating their memories of the events that occurred in their relationship. The letters are not written with the intention of mailing them; indeed, often the teachers to whom they are written are no longer living. Letter writing is used as a literary device to stimulate the memory and to facilitate the recall of specific events and feelings. Some of these letters might be to teachers with whom the person had a positive and life-enhancing experience, some may be to teachers with whom the person had a negative and humiliating experience. A description of the process, which we call the "Dear Teacher" activity, and some examples of letters follow.

Introducing the Activity

Introducing this activity in a class can occur in many different contexts. A class might be discussing the "self" and how it is related to the past and the present, who we are now, and how it relates to how we teach or will teach. The discussion might be centered on the power of feelings of anger, humiliation, disappointment, love, pride, or self-empowerment and how these feelings are alive and powerful in classrooms. The class might be talking about the power of the "hidden" curriculum in the classroom and how it has affected us and how we, in turn, must be aware of the power it will have on our students. The discussion might be focused on values, the ethic of caring, or the power of relationships developed with students. In any of these contexts, the "Dear Teacher" activity serves as a catalyst for students to remember experiences that are relevant in any of these discussions.

It is important to spend time creating the context in which people feel connected to the task and can comfortably make an independent decision about hurtful or caring teachers they have had and to whom their letter should be addressed. If students cannot do this, it is probably for good reason. Don't force them. Help them feel comfortable in not writing, or in writing a different kind of letter, for example, "To my favorite teacher."

Tell people before they start writing that they will be provided an opportunity to read their letters to the group if they choose to do so, but that no one will be embarrassed or required to read. Follow through, being careful that no one feels any obligation to share their letters. Tell people in advance that there may be strong feelings associated with the letters when they are read so that no one is surprised. That will help mitigate the feelings of those who weep or who might otherwise feel strange, out of control, or embarrassed. The feelings expressed in the class when the letters are read can be very similar to the feelings these individuals had when they were children and first experiencing what they are writing about; that is, reliving a painful story.

Although you might vary the script some to fit your own style, one might start the activity in this way:

> We will be doing a little reminiscing today, looking back on some teachers that we have had in the past. We will be looking at two (or three) teachers: (1) ones who may have hurt, shamed, or disappointed us; (2) ones who loved us and had a positive impact on our lives.
>
> There are teachers we all know whose certificates we would like to retroactively suspend. We would like to cancel the time they have spent with children and forbid them from ever being in the presence of children again. They may be teachers who shamed or embarrassed us, failed to acknowledge or support us at an important time, demeaned us, hit us, or were otherwise inappropriate with us. Our most dramatic memory may be what we observed being done to another child rather than ourselves.
>
> Most of us know at least one teacher like that. Names and faces probably come to mind as you think back about your experiences in kindergarten, in elementary school, as an adolescent in middle or high school, or even as an adult at the university. Let me help you by telling a story about one of my own teachers. (Relate a story or two about a teacher who was hurtful to you. Recall the effect as well as the event.)
>
> Now I am going to ask you to think about one of your teachers and take about 15 minutes to write him or her a letter. This is a chance for you to tell him or her what you have always wanted to say. Say it! Plainly! Remember, hurt feelings and angry feelings are very close together. You don't have to justify yourself to anyone, just say in the letter what you want to say. Begin by introducing yourself: "Dear _____, You will remember me, I was the boy/girl who. . . ." Think about who you were then, where you were, and how you were (quiet, rowdy, etc.). Describe what happened that has stuck in your memory. Describe your feelings at the time. Then, "something I have always wanted to tell you is. . . ."
>
> As you write, your affective memory will engage. Let it go and tell the person what you think and feel. This can be a "go-to-hell" letter, or a "how-could-you?" letter, or any kind of letter you choose to write. We're not going to send them, so be as free to write about the experiences as you want.

At this point tell the group that, after about 20 minutes, you will give them the opportunity to share their letters, strictly on a voluntary basis. Assure them that, if they so choose, no one except themselves will see their letters and that this assurance is to free them from any unnecessary constraint on their writing.

It is rather easy to see when most have finished their letters. Often two or three will be so involved in their letter that they will continue. Allow them to finish if possible. If it is taking too much time, suggest that they come to a stopping point as soon as possible and that they may wish to finish it later.

Then, ask for students who wish to share their letters. Suggestions for the sharing time are described below. After students share their letters, introduce the second letter. You might say:

> Now it is time to remember a different kind of teacher, the kind of person we wish our own children could have in school, and every child in the world for that matter. They are teachers who loved us, teachers who cared for us in special ways that imprinted our lives, teachers who were there in a difficult time of our lives. Let me share one of my memories of such a teacher in my life. (Relate an experience with a teacher that had a positive impact on your life. Recall the events and feelings you had at the time as well as your feelings at the moment about that teacher.) Now you can write a letter to this caring teacher; say what you would like to say to someone who cared for you and participated in a significant way in your school career. Again recall how you were at the time, your feelings, perceptions, and needs. Describe what happened and its impact on you.

Sharing the Letters

After about 20 minutes, or when most everyone is finished writing each of the letters, say:

> Okay, who is willing to share their letter with the group? It takes a lot of courage to begin. Let me say that reading these letters can be emotionally very difficult. For that reason, no one should feel coerced to do so. However, sharing what you have written can also be helpful. Hearing the stories of others and having our stories heard by others can be freeing. Feelings are okay. You will not be shamed for them here. Some may have a story they should not share with the class for reasons of privacy or feelings of emotional jeopardy. Don't share it. If you would like and if you feel it would help, I would be happy to meet with you individually and hear you read your letter and discuss it. Who would like to begin?

Then wait. It usually takes a while for the first letter to be read. You may need to encourage someone to begin. You may catch someone's eye who just needs your word of encouragement or a nod to read his or her letter. Frequently, it is necessary to wait for the first person to break the ice. Allow silence; don't feel like you must talk or cajole. Usually someone will volunteer and then others will follow quickly. In our experience, most choose to read their letters and are glad they did. They consistently report feeling good about their experience and for some it is a catharsis.

While people read their letters, it's best to just wait and let them say what they need to. Students will also perhaps get emotional while reading these letters; that is part of the power of the activity. Allow a person time to read and have tissues ready for those who may need it. Silence in a session like this can be very important because often it involves grief and a flood of forgotten memories. Let the experience stand alone for what it is; no one, including the leader, comments or in any way presumes to offer any analysis. Always express appreciation to each person after they finish reading their letter, and if it was a particularly difficult letter for them, acknowledge the courage it took to share.

Again, do *not* push a person or probe any feelings or facts or offer interpretations. All they say "makes sense" to them. You do not necessarily need to understand the sense it makes. If a person becomes frightened, self-conscious, or overly anxious about their feelings or revealing their feelings, direct attention away from the person. You can say, "This can be hard stuff to remember and even harder to read. Maybe you would like to relax for a few minutes while someone else reads your letter." Through eye contact with the group you can usually see someone who is likely to be willing. Don't call on him or her; watch, without manipulating with a "won't you please read" stare, to see if you get a gesture of willingness to read. Keep talking in the meantime. Have another story of your own to share if the group chooses to be totally silent. Close physical proximity to the person who became overly anxious can be helpful when you are making the transition, but moving away from the person can help shift the group's attention away from him/her also, and can provide a modicum of privacy.

Permit humor. Individuals may find in humor some relief for themselves and for the group. As long as there is clearly no possibility that a person will feel laughed at or scoffed, comic relief can be helpful and facilitate moving on.

Discussing the Activity

You might end by discussing the process, again not trying to analyze individual's experiences but in talking about how the students think this relates to their lives as teachers, both professionally and personally. Commonalities across the letters may point to important implications of this activity. Ideas such as the ethic of care, the nature of knowing, and personal philosophy and public behavior of teachers might be part of the discussion.

Major issues emerge in these sessions that have current ethical meaning and moral content. Gender, race, sexual preference, and religious views are examples. Respecting the meaning and profound significance of these issues to those expressing them and protecting them in the group in the process is essential. You may or may not agree, and there may be a member of the group who disagrees. This is not the time for debating the merits of positions. It is only a time for learning to listen to deeply held private stories and respecting the storyteller.

Following are excerpts from letters students have written that illustrate the range of issues raised.

Dear teacher,
Remember me when . . .

I was in your junior high school class. You said something to me that I still remember after twenty years; that you hoped that I would learn respect. Respect is something that I have learned, not in schools, but from the people from which I came. Possibly it was you that needed to learn respect; respect of others' culture . . . [that not all of us] should thank Christopher Columbus . . . for the opportunity at "civilization."

I was in your grade 10 Home Ec. class. You were devoted to your pupils. . . . You always had time to listen to us, both in and out of class.

I was in your first grade class. I still remember the humiliation that very first hour of the first day when you asked where I lived and I replied "at the top of the hill." Your response, "What, in a tree or a cave?" still upsets me. You see, with 17 families sharing my surname, I had been taught to say I lived "at the top of the hill," so that everyone knew which [surname] was my parent.

I was in your grade 10 English class. I sure felt safe to take a risk in your class. I actually tried hard, knowing I might fail, but felt safe enough to do so.

I was in your elementary school class. I remember all the negative things you said about my culture. You taught me to feel inferior because of who I was. You taught me to deny my spiritual beliefs. . . . You deserve to be called ineffective, insensitive, also racist. You should never have had the opportunity to teach any child in this world.

I was in your grade 5 class. You were a new teacher and you worked very hard at making all of us feel special. I worked in my usual quiet way, but you seemed to notice me, even though my class was very large. You made everyone feel they had something to offer. You invited the whole class to the church to see your wedding. [It] was the first time I realized a teacher could be a "person."

[I was in your middle school class]? Probably not! How many times can you remember falling asleep at your desk, or not waking up early enough to arrive at school on time. How many times was it because of the parties you attended the night before? At the time I thought it was great. We could do what we wanted, when we wanted, as long as you weren't there. But now I realize I was cheated [out of] a nurturing stimulating environment. My educational development for nearly one entire year was denied me!

I was in your grade 7 class. . . . add to your lack of ability to generate understanding in your subject area, you were the meanest SOB in the building, bar none. It wasn't any one major event that made me fear you, it was the list of [your] nasty little ways.

I was in your grade 9 class and you praised me for my creative writing. Until that time, I had never thought of myself as a very creative person but your faith in me spurred me on to choose English as my major at the university.

Some things I remember you saying when I was in your grade 3 classroom are: "My you were a pretty baby, too bad you're so fat now"; "Are you too stupid to listen?" and "You're too dumb to remember times tables." All I can say is—Look at me now!

IMPLICATIONS

Stories told in letters written to former teachers contain part of what is remembered of the drama of the classroom. These stories become existential records of what impressed and mattered most, containing the meaning of experiences that would most likely escape the notes of observers who might have been present. It is within the drama that students come to understandings about themselves and others. This is the site of power for teachers in shaping the imagination of students, a site often overlooked in thinking about how and what students learn. Stories about our teachers are mental records of regard—or disregard, or affirmation, or negation—of the value of self in the microcosm of the world that is the classroom. Several important implications of learning about self in the highly storied and powerful acts of teaching and learning are worth noting. Five are mentioned here.

First, teaching is a self-reflecting as well as self-reflective activity. It involves the translation of one's own stories into relationships with students and teacher behavior. How the teacher sees herself and what she tells herself she is doing as a teacher reflects the meaning she has taken from stories in her own life. The issue is not whether or not this is true, but the extent to which the teacher is aware of the impact of the stories that make up her own history on her views and activities as a teacher.

Second, the knowledge base for the teacher's work is his own construction of what he understands to be empirically validated practice, the local culture, and his own values and beliefs about teaching. The teacher's craft is, in this sense, idiosyncratic. Different things are going on in different classrooms even in the same grade in the same school. His craft is personally, as well as professionally, storied. Self-knowledge, therefore, is an important aspect of the teacher's competence in constructing the knowledge base for teaching.

Third, stories influence morals and ethical reasoning. The classroom is saturated with issues of interest such as gender, race, ethnicity, and ability. The teacher's decisions and behavior reflect her position with respect to equity and fairness, for example. Her own values in this regard are revealed in stories about her own life as she experienced and observed the moral behavior of others.

Fourth, the "hidden" curriculum has been acknowledged for decades. More happens than is planned and more than is told. The emotional and social welfare of students is affected by what is implicit, by what is suggested, by subtlety in language, by seating arrangements, by who is called on to answer questions, by who is given special responsibilities, and by who is given recognition. The script for the hidden curriculum is written in the teacher's own stories about teaching and learning in the classroom. Those scripts hold the potential for both care and cruelty.

Fifth, stories have their own power both to nurture and to heal. It is as true for teachers as it is for their students—stories have the power to repair a spirit in disarray (Lopez, 1989). Bringing into awareness the events, along with all the complexity of the contexts in which they occurred in shaping our values and views of ourselves, is a powerful intervention. Various psychotherapies, implemented within particular psychological theories, have had a similar aim.

CONCLUSIONS

The storied letters about caring and cruelty in the classroom reflect the complexity and multidimensionality of good stories. They reveal what is true about experience in the classroom—both what is known and what is hidden. They suggest that what students remember most are their relationships with teachers and their classmates—how they were treated and the feelings they had at the time. The letters gain access to stories of care and cruelty, of the use and abuse of power.

We have described the nature of story and its importance to teaching as the context in which the activity of letter writing is understood. We have suggested that, in our experience, the letter-writing activity is useful in helping teachers remember and have the opportunity to share experiences with cruel and caring teachers that help shape their values and beliefs and now impact their lives as teachers.

REFERENCES

Brockelman, P. (1985). *Time and self.* New York: Crossroads.

Carter, K. (1993). The place of story in the study of teaching and teacher education. *Educational Researcher, 22*(1), 5–12.

Dewey, J. (1916). *Democracy and education: An introduction to the philosophy of education.* New York: Macmillan.

Diamond, C. (1993). Writing to reclaim self: The use of narrative in teacher education. *Teaching and Teacher Education, 9*(5, 6), 511–517.

Grumet, M. R. (1991). The politics of personal knowledge. In C. Witherell & N. Noddings (Eds.), *Stories lives tell: Narrative and dialogue in education.* New York: Teachers College Press.

Hargreaves, A., & Tucker, E. (1991). Teaching and guilt: Exploring the feelings of teaching. *Teaching and Teacher Education, 7*(5, 6), 491–505.

Jackson, P. (1992). Untaught lessons. New York: Teacher's College Press.

Kelchtermans, G. (1993). Getting the story, understanding the lives: From career stories to teachers' professional development. *Teaching and Teacher Education, 9*(5, 6), 443–456.

Lopez, B. (1989). *Crossing open ground.* New York: Vintage Books.

McCutcheon, G. (1992). Facilitating teacher personal theorizing. In E. W. Ross, J. W. Cornett, & G. McCutcheon (Eds.), *Teacher personal theorizing: Connecting curriculum practice, theory and research.* New York: State University of New York Press.

Morrison, T. (1987). The site of memory. In W. Zinsser (Ed.), *Inventing the truth: The art and craft of memoirs* (pp. 101–124). Boston: Houghton Mifflin.

Noblit, G. (1993). Power and caring. *American Educational Research Journal, 30*(1), 23–38.

Noddings, N. (1991). Stories in dialogue: Caring and interpersonal relationships. In C. Witherell & N. Noddings, (Eds.), *Stories lives tell: Narrative and dialogue in education.* New York: Teachers College Press.

Weber, S. (1993). The narrative anecdote in teacher education. *Journal of Education for Teaching, 19*(1), 71–82.

Welty, E. (1984). *One writer's beginnings.* Cambridge: Harvard University Press.

Witherell, C. (1991). The self in narrative: A journey into paradox. In C. Witherell & N. Noddings (Eds.), *Stories lives tell: Narrative and dialogue in education.* New York: Teachers College Press.

Witherell, C., & Noddings, N. (Eds.). (1991). *Stories lives tell: Narrative and dialogue in education.* New York: Teachers College Press.

3

NEGATIVE PEDAGOGY

Karen Colucci
University of South Florida

The physical, emotional, and academic safety of children is entrusted to schools on a daily basis. Schools and school districts plan curriculum and develop policies and programs to meet the obligations of this trust, but are often not cognizant of the full impact of their actions. What starts out as a way to ensure the best interests of the students is implemented only to the "letter of the law"; missing the full intent, or worse yet, becoming diluted with bias and distortions. These practices form negative pedagogy in the schools. Negative pedagogy is a threat to the emotional, intellectual, and physical safety of children. Some negative pedagogy is clearly discernible, but some is so insidious that teachers and students are not even aware of the effects.

This chapter explores some of the areas in which negative pedagogy exists in schools. The purpose is not to expose all of the negative pedagogy in schools or its causes but rather to stimulate self-reflection within our own practice as educators. The beliefs we hold and the underlying assumptions we make as educators color everything we do in schools from the decisions we make and the relationships we form, to the instructional approaches we use. Even caring educators may engage in practices or carry out actions that have a negative impact on students without even realizing it. Therefore, a critical examination of our practices and beliefs can help us become cognizant of the implications of those actions/beliefs and the profound effects they have on students.

A helpful heuristic to examine negative pedagogy and its effects consists of the categories of the formal, informal, and hidden curriculum. These categories are not static; they overlap, are connected, and may change over time; they provide a starting point for the examination of practices in classrooms and schools. The formal curriculum is comprised of the stated practices, policies, and goals of schools. It is apparent to all those in the school community. Very little negative pedagogy exists here because of the careful scrutiny and exposure the formal curriculum is receives. When the nation's attention is focused on education, it is focused here. One of the exceptions is corporal punishment. Despite the call for its demise by many professional organizations and child advocates, corporal punishment still exists as a formal, written discipline policy in some areas of the country. On the surface, corporal punishment is a threat to the physical safety of children. This type of punishment can result in serious physical injury such as circulatory or nervous system damage as well as broken bones (Taylor & Maurer, 1985). The damage can also go much deeper into the emotional well-being of the child. This damage is not as obvious as a physical injury but can be just as debilitating (Simmons, 1991). Corporal punishment also extends into the hidden curriculum through the messages it sends to children such as "force is preferred over reasoning" (Simmons, 1991). It is a form of physical coercion that creates a definite division of power between adults and children, leaving children feeling powerless. We can no longer risk the physical and emotional safety of children based solely on tradition or the perceived absence of other effective disciplinary approaches. We have the obligation to examine the effects of corporal punishment in terms of the intended outcomes and the assumptions we make about its use.

Related to the formal curriculum is the informal curriculum. It is not formal written policy, but is part of the conscious actions of teachers and schools. It may be "unspoken or unwritten rules," owned biases or deliberate unwritten plans of action. Students are often aware of the informal curriculum but their awareness is not a criterion of its existence. Most of the negative pedagogy in the informal curriculum centers on a school's or teacher's conscious beliefs about groups of students and how they learn and behave. For example, a teacher who believes that students who live in economically depressed areas have inferior intellectual abilities might not put as much effort into planning instruction for those children. S/he might justify this action by saying, "They won't learn no matter what I do, so why bother?"

Another example of negative pedagogy in the informal curriculum is the segregation of students. Students who are labeled emotionally or behaviorally handicapped or severely emotionally disturbed are often segregated from other students in the school and are not permitted to engage in most schoolwide activities (Knitzer, Steinberg, & Fleisch, 1990). The reason given for this segregation is often due to an open bias against these students. Statements such as, "They are animals" or "They can't be trusted" are often voiced. The statements given for both examples hint at underlying fears. Fears of not being successful in facilitating the learning of these students and fears of perceived chaotic situations instigated by these students. Fear is a powerful emotion and unless it is exposed and resolved, it continues to color the actions of the person who holds it. Bias driven by fear is often difficult to uncover and confront because it precipitates defensive actions and words. Therefore, when bias is suspected in our own actions or those around us it is more effectively dealt with through critical examination rather than accusations. Accusations fuel the fires of defensiveness and drive bias and fear further "underground." We must be diligent in our efforts and gather the resolve to be honest with ourselves and our colleagues continually asking, "What am I afraid of?" or "What are we as a group afraid of?" Once fear is exposed, it can be addressed in a supportive environment in which diverse options are explored, information is gathered, and implications for possible solutions are examined. We can no longer afford to ignore this part of pedagogy in schools; the emotional, academic, and physical safety of students depend on it.

The third area in which negative pedagogy can be found within schools is in the hidden curriculum. The hidden curriculum is the most nebulous and subtle of the three. Those in the school community are usually not aware of its existence or its effects. The hidden curriculum consists of the unwritten and unspoken biases, practices, ideas, and philosophies of teachers, schools, and school districts. Although it is not always negative, when it is, its damage can be far reaching because of its insidious nature.

The types of negative pedagogy in the hidden curriculum are numerous. They are also arguably the most devastating due to the deep wounds they inflict on the physical, emotional, and academic safety of students. These wounds are seldom obvious and their effects are often masked. For purposes of examination in this chapter, negative pedagogy within the hidden curriculum is clustered into the following categories: discipline and relationships with students; evaluation of students; grouping of students; classroom/school procedures and rules; methods of instruction; and physical plant/resources.

DISCIPLINE AND RELATIONSHIPS WITH STUDENTS

Dear Mr. Keller,

I'm writing this to tell you of a tremendous impact you had on me during 5th grade. I'll never forget the day when you made Jimmy come to the front of the room and stand on one foot—then badgered him, telling him to lift both feet at the same time until finally, tears streaming down his face, he did lift both feet at once and fell to the floor.

Now, Jimmy was not a very good student and not well liked by us children, but that was a horrible, humiliating, degrading, cruel way for you to show this boy that you disapproved of his behavior. I remember feeling angry at you and quite frankly, nothing short of horrified. What an awful way to treat that little boy! Now that I'm a teacher, I'd just like to thank you for showing me how *not* to do it!

Your Former Student,
Mary

Many teachers see the role of discipline as being a behavior control device rather than a learning and teaching tool (Nelsen, 1993). It is doubtful, however, that teachers enter the profession because it provides opportunities to control others (Nichols, 1992). Often, issues of control related to discipline emerge when teachers are faced with orchestrating the classroom learning environment for the diversity of learners that exist in schools today. As student populations become more and more diverse, and as students are impacted and influenced by changes within our society, the behavioral responses and patterns that students bring to the classroom also become diverse and may be perceived as challenging. Teachers who are unable to understand and embrace the diversity in positive ways are left with very few options. When faced with complex problems and situations, teachers tend to react in ways that are consistent with their own experience (Goodman,1988; Hollingsworth, 1989; Lortie, 1975; Zeichner & Tabachnick, 1985). In other words, they teach the way they were taught. If a teacher's own learning experiences included classrooms in which the learners were not diverse and everyone was expected to act and react in the same way, that might very well be their schema for "classroom." Therefore, when faced with diversity in the classroom, in order to make everyone conform and act/react in the same way, control becomes a comfortable option. The use of control as a discipline approach is further reinforced by administrators and colleagues who make remarks such as, "She is such a good teacher. She has such control over the students. You can hear a pin drop in her room."

When a teacher sets herself/himself up as the controlling force in a classroom, it effectively puts up a wall between the students and the teacher (Dollard, Christensen, Colucci, & Epanchin, 1996). When teachers are unable to develop positive relationships with students, they are limited in the ways in which they can interact with students. This type of system also hampers communication in a classroom because teachers invariably, due to the role they have set up, "talk down" to students. When you construct a role for yourself in which everyone around you is subordinate, communication patterns take on authoritative, subordinate characteristics (Edwards, 1980).

Controlling environments can hamper student learning and can actually exacerbate the behaviors that the teacher intended to control (Nichols, 1992). Further, the use of rewards and punishment (the traditional mainstay of control based discipline approaches) can be perceived as coercive and can impede a student's development of personal responsibility for his/her actions (Kohn, 1996). When teachers put themselves "in charge" of controlling student behavior, students come to rely on that. They act or perform in the way the teacher expects in order to get a reward or avoid a punishment. However, when the controlling force (the teacher) is no longer there, the student is at a loss in terms of self-control, mediating differences with others, and dealing with emotionally charged situations. They have not been instructed in how to problem-solve in order to deal with challenging situations and have not been given any practice in self-control. Teachers often justify control-based discipline approaches by saying, "I am teaching self-control by helping the student act in appropriate ways. Reinforcing positive behaviors and punishing negative behaviors will help the student internalize positive behaviors and extinguish negative behaviors." What tends to happen, however, is that the student internalizes how to get the reward or avoid the punishment rather than developing self-control and responsible behavior (Kohn, 1996).

Teacher power used to control is not always negative, however. George Noblit (1993), uses the term "moral authority" to describe a teacher's use of power and control to ensure the academic, emotional, and physical safety of all within the community of the classroom. He also makes the distinction between power and oppression. Power, when used within the context of moral authority, is closely linked with caring and respect. Oppression is the absence of caring and takes place within the context of a nonreciprocal relationship. Teacher power used to help students develop responsibility for their own actions can be positive if the teacher engages the student in problem solving, instructs the student in possible alternatives to problem behavior, and empowers the student to make choices and decisions about his/her own actions.

Discipline is often touted as a means to protect the physical, academic, and emotional safety of students in the classroom. However, if we do not carefully consider the effects of the decisions we make and actions we take in the name of discipline, the very student safety we seek to protect may be jeopardized.

EVALUATION OF STUDENTS

Dear Mr. James,

I was in your 10th grade math class. I am writing to let you know how your attitude and teaching methods have affected me. Many times, you rattled off formulas etc. so quickly that if I failed to understand you, and tried to think about what you had said, I lost track and became completely lost. After asking you to please explain more fully how to do the equation, I was spoken to like I was completely stupid. The one thing I did learn was not to ask for help in any of my classes; it was just too humiliating in front of my peers.

I can even remember going to you after class one day and making an appointment to see you after school. When the time came, I was there, but clearly you were uninterested. You completely ignored me and continued to write the next day's lesson on the board. I tried to speak up. You knew I was there, but the fear of you and your superior attitude kept me from saying very much. I left no more enlightened mathematically than when I'd arrived and I continued to fail your tests.

To this day, I feel inadequate when it comes to math. That feeling kept me from attempting algebra and routed me into a general math class. That closed a lot of doors that I had always hoped would be open to me.

It also kept me from taking chemistry because you were teaching it. Your belief that the truly intelligent people would always do well on your tests and in your class is frankly foul. For years, I had little belief in myself. As an adult, I took my first university class - English. It was there that I finally learned my gifts and that I had more than mush for brains.

In your single-mindedness and need to be right, you missed out on that.

Your Former Student,
Debbie

Negative pedagogy in the category of evaluation centers on using evaluation as an end in and of itself. Evaluation becomes a tool of stratification and a means of finding deficits in children. Grades and test scores become flags of failure instead of a call for instruction that better matches the student's needs. Raffini (1993) reports that, "There appears to be wide agreement among students, parents, and educators that the grades of A and B are the only valid designators of school achievement; they are also used to reward the behaviors that produce it" (p. 182). These behaviors are also often narrowly defined and do not take into account individual differences. Raffini goes on to say,

> Structures that must inadvertently produce academic losers as a by-product in the creation of academic winners motivate only those who believe they have a reasonable chance of ending up near the top. . . . we should not be surprised when large numbers decide to either physically or psychologically withdraw from participation. (p. 182)

In the area of norm-referenced testing, we send many messages to children about what is valued in schools. Intelligence tests have long been used in education to sort students and place them in various groups and categories. The tests of intelligence we use clearly value linguistic and analytic types of skills. Those students that do not possess skills and talents in these areas are then given the message that what they know and can do is not valued. They might be talented athletes, musicians, or leaders, but the talent and knowledge they possess is seldom acknowledged in a meaningful or equitable way. This message is further reinforced by the reduced amount of instructional time allocated to music, art, drama, and physical education in schools, as compared to other subject areas (Goodlad, 1984). Instruction in these "nonacademic" areas is also the first to be eliminated if there is a shortage of resources or time in the schools.

Howard Gardner (1983) has brought the issue of multiple intelligences to the forefront and suggests that we need to acknowledge, encourage, and reward intelligences and the development of intelligences in all areas including, but not limited to, spatial, interpersonal, intrapersonal, musical, bodily kinesthetic, linguistic, and logical-mathematical. He also suggests that the talents and knowledge that students possess in these areas might serve as an entree for instruction into subject matter where they may not be as strong (Gardner, 1991).

The use of objective criterion-referenced testing as a means to assign a grade or document mastery also sends many messages to students. First, it sends messages about the worth of the individual. Most students equate their self-worth in schools with their achievements in schools (Raffini, 1993). When a student receives an "F" on a test it is deemed as his/her failure. Seldom is the appropriateness or quality of the instruction questioned. Secondly, it sends the message that there is always one "correct" answer. When the student responds with anything else, the answer is incorrect. For example, a student responded to the following test question, "If you had two apples and lost one of them, how many would you have?" with the answer, "a half." She reasoned that if she only had one apple she would have to share it with her brother and would be left with "a half." This answer was, of course, marked incorrect, the "correct" answer being one. We often applaud this type of evaluation as being objective and fair, however, this type of evaluation does not get at the reasoning process of students or their real understanding of the subject matter. It also sends false messages to the students about mastery. If a student receives an "A" on a test, they are credited with mastering the material covered by the test even though they may have only memorized enough information to answer the test questions correctly. These messages impact a student's ideas about learning and knowledge. In an interview with Ron Brandt (1993), Howard Gardner states:

> Most schools have fallen into a pattern of giving kids exercises and drills that result in their getting answers on tests that look like understanding. It's what I call the "correct answer compromise": students read a text, they take a test, and everybody agrees that if they say a certain thing it'll be counted as understanding.
>
> But the findings of cognitive research over the past 20–30 years are really quite compelling: students do not understand, in the most basic sense of that term. That is, they lack the capacity to take knowledge learned in one setting and apply it appropriately in a different setting. Study after study has found that, by and large, even the best students in the best schools can't do that. (p. 4)

If learning and understanding are equated in the student's mind with memorization and the type of mastery depicted above then the use of lifelong learning as a tool for personal development is not a likely outcome.

GROUPING OF STUDENTS

Dear Mrs. Simms,

I was a student in your 10th grade remedial math class. The rest of my classmates and I often wondered why you ever became a teacher. You never had a smile on your face and you were quick to put students in what you thought was their place. I got the impression that we were wasting your time. After all, we were in one of the lowest math classes. If you could come to school, drink your coffee, and not be bothered you would have probably preferred it. I do want to thank you for giving me a good example of how not to teach.

What bothered me most was how you embarrassed some of the students who did not perform well. I am sure your style turned more than a few students off to school.

Your Former Student,
Mike

The way we group students for instruction can result in effects that many may not be aware of. Ability or homogeneous grouping is one such example. Despite much research exposing the ills of this practice, it is still instituted in many schools throughout the country (Hereford, 1993; Kozol, 1991). Not only do students pick up on who is the "dumb" group and who is the "smart" group, they internalize this message. As Raffini (1993) states, "Few adults who have never been branded with the 'below label' can appreciate the impact of the label on the self-worth of those forced to accept it." He goes on to state, "Even the label 'average' can be devastating to many students" (p. 6). Students also come to internalize behavior that is attributed to below-average groups, "Clearly, many politicians, parents, and students have come to believe that the label 'below average' on any measure of academic achievement indicates that one is incompetent, lazy, or unambitious" (Raffini, 1993, p. 47).

Ability grouping sends even more subtle messages related to attribution. There is often an overrepresentation of culturally diverse children and children of poverty in the "lower" groups due to biased testing and placement procedures (Hereford, 1993). Lower academic achievement then becomes equated with membership in a minority or socioeconomic group, thus creating a downward spiral of bias. In an environment of bias and condemnation, every child's emotional safety is at risk.

An often cited rationale for ability or homogeneous grouping is : "If you reduce the range of abilities among a group of students, it will be easier for a teacher to target instruction to meet those students' needs, thus, all of the students will achieve more" (Hereford, 1993, p. 50). Research has not supported this rationale (Goodlad, 1984; Hereford, 1993; Kagan, 1992). In a meta- analysis of 65 studies, it was found that students from classes that included heterogeneous peer tutoring out-performed those from control classes (Kagan, 1992).

In a related vein, Goodlad (1984), found that effective instructional practices were more often the norm in "higher" ability groups rather than "lower" ability groups. He found that with the "higher" groups, teachers were more enthusiastic, more organized, and clearer in their expectations. Goodlad further characterizes the "lower" group as "educationally disadvantaged" (p. 157). This type of teacher behavior sends a hidden message to those students in the "lower" groups, "You are not important to me and neither is your academic achievement."

The issue of grouping students also opens the question of access to knowledge. If students are not provided with an effective instructional environment, their access to knowledge is limited and instructional practices become a means of perpetuating difference in academic achievement (Freire & Horton, 1990; Giroux, 1983; Goodlad, 1984;). Students caught in this cycle are put at risk emotionally as well as academically.

CLASSROOM/SCHOOL PROCEDURES AND RULES

Dear Mrs. Roberts,

You may not remember me but, I was in your 3rd grade class. I was the one that you put masking tape across my mouth and placed on a stool in your metal coat closet and shut the door. I can remember that coat closet as if it were yesterday. It was big, brown, and sat next to your desk. It smelled good, like you, but it was dark from the inside. There was just enough room for a small stool because you had your coat hanging there.

I'm writing this letter to tell you how much you hurt me when you did that to me. I really loved you and you hurt my feelings terribly when you made me get on that stool in the closet. I didn't think that you liked me anymore. You embarrassed me in front of my friends and they teased me about it for a long time. Even though I could hear what was going on, and could see a little bit of light around the door, I have never felt so alone as I did that day. All because I was talking to my girlfriend about the assignment we were completing. Wasn't there something else you could have done? Why was discussing the assignment so bad? It seemed like you never let us talk to each other about anything.

I fell asleep in the closet and you forgot me when it was time for me to go home. My baby-sitter called the school when I didn't get off the bus. You ended up having to take me home and you wrote a letter of apology to my mom. My mom wanted to sue you and the school but the school counselor told her how much work she would have to miss (my mom was the sole support for the five of us and couldn't afford to miss work) and how much attorney fees would be. So the incident was forgotten. But, I never forgot it!

Now that I'm a teacher, I let my students talk about many things. I think it helps them learn. That is something I wish you would have done.

Your Former Student,
Janice

Procedures and rules within classrooms and schools have the power to limit the intellectual and social growth of students. They also have the potential to affect the relationships between adults and students and between students and students. Negative pedagogy in this area is far reaching but seldom contemplated or even recognized.

Rules that limit peer interaction are one example of how the growth of students can be impeded in schools. The control of noise and chaos is often cited as a reason for limiting student interactions. We must be cognizant, however, that noise does not always equal chaos, and rules and techniques to "control the masses" do not always produce an environment that is conducive to learning. Students' active engagement with peers, resources, and teachers in learning environments helps stimulate academic growth in students (Gardner, 1991; Goodlad, 1984; Newman & Wehlage, 1993; Sharan & Sharan, 1990). Having students discuss, contemplate, debate, and explore together may create lively interactions, but seldom chaotic ones if thoughtfully facilitated.

Rules and procedures (or their absence) that restrict peer interaction limit a student's ability to learn about relationship building, interpersonal communication, problem solving, ethics in social situations, celebrating diversity, and cooperation just to name a few. We often institute these rules and procedures without awareness of the consequences or effects. After all, "Students are in school to learn not to socialize and play!" Some examples of these types of rules and procedures are: no talking in the lunchroom, no planned time for peer interaction, little or no cooperative planning of school activities that engage all students, and little or no discussions within classrooms or schools that involve real life social problems.

We also limit the social, emotional, and intellectual growth of students by not allowing them to make choices in schools. We expect students to be responsible and make good decisions but we seldom give guidance or experiences in this area. Consequently, very mixed messages are sent to students that can result in rebellion or even apathy (Raffini, 1993). Empowering learners can be a very frightening proposition to those who feel that part of their role in a school is to maintain a tradition of institutional order. Often the need to control (as previously stated) is not seeded in a overt need for power, but rather a fear of chaos, a fear of not achieving stated goals and objectives, and a fear of not upholding perceived traditions within schools. Our fears need to be confronted and we should take comfort in the fact that even empowered learners need guidance and direction. By allowing students to make genuine choices about their learning and what happens to them in schools, we bring them a step closer to becoming productive members of this society. This does not mean that we should cast students to the wind in an "anything goes" fashion. Rather, it means giving students guidance and a realm of possibilities and choices within guidelines they can handle.

The emotional well-being of students is another area affected by school and classroom procedures and rules. Again, we are seldom aware of the effects of our actions in this area or the messages we send to students. Procedures that point out differences among students and reinforce the notion that different equals deficient can have very debilitating effects. We openly identify students who qualify for a free lunch and use this as an accounting procedure or even as a research tool to determine socioeconomic class. Names are called in lunch lines and it becomes common knowledge among students as to who receives a free lunch and who does not. Students in this classification become stigmatized and are often the brunt of other students' cruel jokes and comments. It also sends the message to students that it is acceptable to classify someone according to their socioeconomic situation and make decisions about them based on this classification.

Differences among students are also pointed out by openly labeling students identified for special education services. Within general education classrooms, schedules for students who receive special educational services are often posted on the board. Teachers who are understandably overwhelmed by the complexity of the schedules they must follow, use the posted schedules as a reminder of when their students with disabilities must leave the classroom for special education services. They are often unaware of the consequences. Even when the other students in the class start calling out, "Eric, its time for you to go to the learning disabilities class," or quietly make disparaging remarks such as, "Susan, its time to go to the retard class," the schedules continue to be posted. Singling out a student in this way can be humiliating for the student. Derogatory names such as "boom-boom" and "retard" affect the self-esteem of students and the emotional safety of the classroom environment is jeopardized.

Singling out students in classrooms also occurs in other ways. The common practice of posting mastery charts or completion charts in classrooms sends messages of comparison and competition to students. Students who are slower to master skills or complete assignments are stigmatized. Also, some students become fearful of helping others with assignments because the student they help may jump ahead of them on the chart. Before long, the star on the chart becomes paramount in the student's mind rather than what they have learned or mastered (Kohn, 1996). Although teachers usually intend to use charts and displays for the purposes of motivating students, they are seldom aware of all of the effects of this practice.

Rules and procedures, or rather the lack thereof, can also be a threat to the physical well-being of students. Violence perpetrated on students by other students is one such example. When schools do not take incidents or threats of violence seriously or do not use these incidents as an opportunity to create a guided dialogue between students in an effort to resolve underlying issues, they do not live up to their responsibility for ensuring the physical safety of students (Hazler, Hoover, & Oliver, 1993). This lack of meaningful action also sends a message to the students that they or their physical safety are not important. We cannot be complacent by saying, "Hindsight is 20/20." We must continually examine our practices, rules, and procedures by asking, "Are we doing all we can to promote positive student relationships, to recognize and meet emotional/social needs of students, and to help students be sensitive to their own biases and constructively work against prejudice?" Our lack of vigilance in this area can have dire consequences for the physical as well as the emotional safety of students in schools.

Another area in which the lack of positive and proactive procedures can send negative messages and negative outcomes is that of family involvement in the schools. If there is no genuine and conscious procedure for meaningful involvement of families in schools, it sends a message to families that their ideas and their cultures are not important at school (Finders & Lewis, 1994). Schools often have ways and procedures for involving families, however, these procedures will continue to be meaningless tokens until schools start understanding families and start involving them in ways that families and students find meaningful (Comer, 1988; Epstein, 1984; McLaughlin & Shields, 1987).

INSTRUCTIONAL PRACTICES

Dear Mr. Tiller,

I was in your 11th grade biology class. I loved science and biology until I took your class. You gave me a great disdain for the subject. Your teaching methods bored the class to tears. We read each chapter out loud at the beginning of the week and spent the rest of the week working quietly on the questions at the end of the chapter along with the endless dittos you passed out. We never discussed anything and you never taught us anything. We were graded on how well we could come up with the answers you thought were right and heaven forbid if we did not head our paper using the "correct" format. I think the only thing I learned in your class was conformity.

I wanted to be a marine biologist but, since you taught marine biology also, I never took the class. My interest in the area waned and I ended up going into another career. I often wonder though, how my life would have been different had I had a biology teacher that would have sparked and sustained my interest rather than squelch it.

Your Former Student,
Kathy

There are many instructional practices commonly used in the schools that have the potential to negatively affect the academic and emotional growth and safety of students. Teachers continue to use these practices because they are not aware of the effects these practices have on students or the messages they send to students. Practices that emphasize conformity among students are one such example. These strategies are often born out of the idea that there is one "right" way to do something or are implemented in the name of teaching children to follow directions. Requiring that all leaves be colored green, all papers be headed in the same way, all math problems be solved using the same procedure and sequence, all student writing follow the same form, and that all students practice the same skills using the same methods and materials are but a few examples. These practices send a message to students that individuality and creativity are not valued. Students who have difficulty conforming in any of the areas, due to a learning difference, may begin to think that there is something wrong with them, that they are not "normal." Teachers must realize that when they emphasize conformity above all else they do not meet the individual needs of all students and jeopardize the academic safety of students.

Another practice that jeopardizes the academic safety and growth of students is the use of instructional methods and materials that are not relevant to students' lives or grounded in their experiences. Some examples are:

1. The use of textbooks that ignore examples, issues, and histories of all but the dominant class of society and instructional methods that do not encourage the examination of multiple perspectives.
2. Classroom discussions of "current events" that don't touch on the controversial issues that students face and do not engage students in critically examining those issues.
3. The use of contrived scenarios to teach social skills such as "getting along with others" while ignoring the surrounding issues such as ongoing disagreements and fights within the classroom.

Practices like these send messages to students that their experiences, backgrounds, and cultures are not valued or important. Further, it jeopardizes the academic growth and safety of students by not providing them with instruction that they can relate to and learn from (Poplin & Weeres, 1992).

Another type of common instructional practice with negative implications is the practice that recognizes the teacher as the keeper of knowledge that s/he is responsible for "pouring" over the students. This practice assumes that by "pouring" this knowledge over the students they will readily absorb it. Lectures, reading from textbooks, and countless worksheets of drill and practice are standard fare within this instructional approach. There is seldom meaningful dialogue between teachers and students, students are seldom active participants in their learning, and there are few opportunities to apply or practice skills or knowledge in meaningful, relevant ways. This approach is long in tradition and many institute it daily without reflecting on the messages that it sends or the effects that it has. Some of the messages that it sends are: there is only one way of knowing; there is a finite number of facts and bits of information that can and should be learned; learning is passive not active; learning is not an independent activity but rather one that only emanates from "experts"; students' ideas and strategies for learning are not important; and knowledge and meaning are static and not constructed. This type of instruction (Gardner, 1991; Newman & Wehlage, 1993; Prawat, 1992; Smith, Smith, & Romberg, 1993) restricts the academic growth of students. Newman and Wehlage (1993) use the term "authentic achievement" to define the type of achievement students make when:

1. Students construct meaning and produce knowledge.
2. Students use disciplined inquiry to construct meaning.
3. Students aim their work toward production of discourse, products, and performances that have value or meaning beyond success in school. (p. 8)

Newman and Wehlage (1993) further state that the instructional approach that supports this type of achievement is grounded in "Five standards of authentic instruction": "higher-order thinking, depth of knowledge, connectedness to the world beyond the classroom, substantive conversation, social support for student achievement" (p. 8). These points are seldom a part of the traditional lecture approach to instruction.

The segregation of subject areas for instructional purposes is another common instructional practice within schools that has negative implications for students. Teachers may argue that this gives them a chance to delve deeply into each subject and give it "its proper attention." They may not be aware, however, what this says to students. For example, it gives students unrealistic expectations and fails to prepare them for a world of complex problems that encompass many disciplines. Seldom in life do you use a skill learned in one discipline or subject area in isolation. We teach in this segregated manner and then wonder why students cannot synthesize, analyze, and apply information.

Lastly, and possibly more importantly, the instructional approaches and procedures we use send messages to students about learning in general and color their academic growth for the future. Many students find school boring and irrelevant (Poplin & Weeres, 1992). Some of the possible reasons for this have been detailed above. Other reasons may lie in specific practices that teachers use, in the name of appropriate instruction. These include practices such as: having the students go through textbooks page by page and problem by problem; over-correction of errors such as having the students write words missed on spelling tests ten times each; paper and pencil drills that take up a majority of class time and have no relevant application; homework that is tedious and has little relevance to the student's life; the requirement that a skill be over-practiced even if it is already mastered such as completing 50 long division problems when the student demonstrated mastery after completing 10; and demanding that all student writing be errorless in structure and mechanics. These practices send messages to students that learning is tedious, not relevant to life experiences, and generally boring. Many students may even develop apathy for learning (Oberlin, 1982; Raffini, 1993). Instead of ensuring academic success and emphasizing the importance of lifelong learning, our practices may in fact ensure academic failure and disdain for learning.

PHYSICAL SCHOOL PLANT/RESOURCES

Dear Mr. Jackson,

You probably won't remember me, but you were the principal of the elementary school I attended. It was a neighborhood school and most of the children that attended the school walked there everyday. Most of the people that lived in our neighborhood were poor, including my family. We did not live in an expensive home and many times, we had trouble making ends meet.

What bothered me was the lack of sensitivity that you and many of the teachers showed for the students and the families. You always drove up to school in your expensive car dressed in your three-piece suit. Your office had beautiful furniture and framed artwork on the wall while us students were in classrooms sitting in desks that were falling apart. Paint in the hallways was peeling and the bathrooms were disgusting. We never had enough textbooks so the students had to share. You and the secretary in the office were the only ones in the school to have a computer.

I can remember you standing in the hallway in the mornings telling the boys to tuck in their shirts because they looked like slobs. I also remember coming to your office to show you a report on Africa that I had completed. My teacher said that since I had done such a good job on it, I should share it with you. When I entered your office, you would not let me sit down on the upholstered chair in your office but, rather made me stand while you looked at the report. After quickly glancing at it, you told me I did a good job, but it would have been better if I had typed it. How could I? I did not have access to a typewriter or a computer.

I felt that you and most of the teachers were there just to get a paycheck. You never really cared about us students and that hurt.

A Former Student,
Jason

Although the physical environment that we surround students with in schools is not typically something that is identified as a part of pedagogy, it can affect how students feel about school and themselves. There are school buildings throughout the country that are dilapidated, poorly ventilated, poorly lit, barren, or even contain substances that are hazardous to human health (Kozol, 1991). When students are surrounded by these conditions on a daily basis, they begin to feel that school is not a nice place to be (Kozol, 1991; Poplin & Weeres, 1992). Students may see other schools that are clean, beautiful, and well-kept within their own city and begin to wonder about the inequity. They interpret these inequities in terms of their own self-worth and begin to believe that school administrators and faculty do not care about their well-being (Kozol, 1991; Poplin & Weeres, 1992).

Resources within schools (or the lack thereof) such as computers, equipment, and learning materials send the same messages to students as the physical school plant. Lack of funding has long been a justification for inequities between schools. There are also insensitive statements such as, "Well, the environment they have at school isn't any different from the environment they have at home, they should be used to it." A pedagogy of caring, seeing value and worth in every individual, and wanting to provide nurturance and the best for each individual would not allow inequities. Although the hurdles to improving physical school plants and resources are large, recognizing inequalities, developing a pedagogy of care within schools, and involving students, families, communities, and business in problem solving are steps well taken.

SUMMARY

The types of negative pedagogy detailed above are not intended to be an exhaustive listing. The chapter does, however, intend to expose the many areas that affect the emotional, academic, and physical well-being of students in schools. The full extent of the effects of practices used in schools is seldom recognized. The messages they send to students are so insidious that even teachers instituting these practices are unaware of them.

There are numerous approaches to teaching and learning, each with their own set of assumptions and implications. Research has shown that there is no one best approach, therefore, we need to examine our practices critically and reflect on the implications they have for students. The philosophies we hold and assumptions we make guide and affect our actions and decisions in schools. The effects of our actions and decisions in turn have profound effects on students.

The "Dear Teacher" letters in this book speak to those effects and the power teachers have in terms of students' lives.

The fact that negative pedagogy exists in the schools should not be as alarming as our failure to recognize it. The often insidious nature of negative practice should not lead us to complacency. We need to acknowledge its presence and the effects it has on students. We must also work to identify its sources and provide for solutions. Reform and restructuring of education are on the lips of the nation. However, until we take a critical look at the underlying philosophies and implications of our actions as educators, all reform and restructuring will be just a reshuffling of old practices. Negative pedagogy will remain an insidious part of our practice and we will continue to provide educational experiences that threaten the emotional and physical safety, as well as the intellectual growth, of children.

REFERENCES

Brandt, R. (1993). On teaching for understanding: A conversation with Howard Gardner. *Educational Leadership, 50*(7), 4–7.

Comer, J. (1988). Educating poor minority children. *Scientific American, 259*(5), 42–48.

Dollard, N., Christensen, L., Colucci, K., & Epanchin, B. (1996). Constructive classroom management. *Focus on Exceptional Children, 29*(2), 1–12.

Edwards, A. D. (1980). Patterns of power and authority in classroom talk. In P. Woods (Ed.), *Teacher strategies*. London: Croom Helm.

Epstein, J. (1984). School policy and parent involvement: Research results. *Educational Horizons, Winter*, 70–72.

Finders, M., & Lewis, C. (1994). Why some parents don't come to school. *Educational Leadership, 51*(8), 50–54.

Freire, P., & Horton, M. (1990). *We make the road by walking*. Philadelphia: Temple University Press.

Gardner, H. (1983). *Frames of mind*. New York: Basic Books.

Gardner, H. (1991). *The unschooled mind*. New York: Basic Books.

Giroux, H. (1983). *Theory and resistance in education*. New York: Bergin & Garvey.

Goodlad, J. (1984). *A place called school*. New York: McGraw-Hill.

Goodman, J. (1988). Constructing a practical philosophy of teaching: A study of preservice teachers' perspectives. *Teaching and Teacher Education, 4*(2), 121–137.

Hazler, R. J., Hoover, J. H., & Oliver, R. (1993). What do kids say about bullying? *The Education Digest, 58*(7), 16–20.

Hereford, N. (1993). Making sense of ability grouping. *Instructor Magazine, 102*(9), 50–52.

Hollingsworth, S. (1989). Prior beliefs and cognitive change in learning to teach. *American Education Research Journal, 26*, 160–189.

Kagan, S. (1992). *Cooperative learning*. California: Resources for Teachers.

Knitzer, J., Steinberg, Z., & Fleisch, B. (1990). *At the schoolhouse door*. New York: Bank Street College of Education.

Kohn, A. (1996). *Beyond discipline: From compliance to community*. Alexandria, VA: Association for Supervision and Curriculum Development.

Kozol, J. (1991). *Savage inequalities: Children in America's schools*. New York: Holt, Rinehart & Winston.

Lortie, D. C. (1975). *Schoolteacher: A sociological study*. Chicago, IL: The University of Chicago Press.

McLaughlin, M., & Shields, P. (1987, October). Involving low-income parents in the schools: A role for policy? *Phi Delta Kappan, 88*, 156–160.

Nelsen, J. (1993). *Positive discipline in the classroom*. Rocklin, CA: Prima Publishers.

Newman, F., & Wehlage, G. (1993). Five standards of authentic instruction. *Educational Leadership, 50*(7), 8–21.

Nichols, P. (1992). The curriculum of control: Twelve reasons for it, some arguments against it. *Beyond Behavior, 3*, 5–11.

Noblit, G. (1993). Power and caring. *American Educational Research Journal, 30*(1), 23–38.

Oberlin, L. (1982). How to teach children to hate mathematics. *School Science and Mathematics, 82*, 261.

Poplin, M., & Weeres, J. (1992). *Voices from within*. Claremont, CA: The Institute for Education in Transformation at The Claremont Graduate School.

Prawat, R. (1992). Teacher' beliefs about teaching and learning: A constructivist perspective. *American Journal of Education, May*, 354–395.

Raffini, J. (1993). *Winners without losers*. Needham Heights, MA: Allyn and Bacon.

Sharan, Y., & Sharan, S. (1990). Group investigation expands cooperative learning. *Educational Leadership, 46*, 17–21.

Simmons, B. (1991). Ban the hickory stick. *Childhood Education, 68*(2), 69–70.

Smith, S., Smith, M., & Romberg, T. (1993). What the NCTM standards look like in one classroom. *Educational Leadership, 50*(8), 4–18.

Taylor, L., & Maurer, A. (1985). *Think twice: The medical effects of physical punishment.* Berkeley, CA: Generation Books.

Zeichner, K., & Tabachnick, B. (1985). The development of teacher perspectives: Social strategies and institutional control in the socialization of beginning teachers. *Journal of Education for Teaching, 11*(1), 1–25.

4

CARING PEDAGOGY

James L. Paul
University of South Florida

Karen Colucci
University of South Florida

In the previous chapter, Colucci's discussion of negative pedagogy focused on the enormous complexity of relationships in the classroom and the ways in which children can be harmed. However noble the intentions, uninformed and thoughtless classroom activities and teacher behaviors can have devastating consequences for children. By contrast, caring pedagogy can help heal a child wounded by humiliation, and it can create or restore self confidence needed for participating in the positive learning opportunities in the classroom. It can also help form the moral foundations of responsible citizenship, productive community membership and leadership, and lifelong engagement in learning.

Caring pedagogy exists in a complex social network of relationships in the classroom and the school. The relationships among teachers, students, teaching methods, curricula, and the culture in the classroom and school afford unlimited opportunities for students to learn about themselves as being good and worthy or as bad and unfit. We have known for many years that the intended curricula—our objectives and methods—account for only part of what a student experiences in school and sometimes not even the part that most affects the student's sense of self-worth and competence.

In this chapter, we first examine the recent philosophical context of educators' interest in caring pedagogy. We then examine the power of caring relationships with teachers as remembered by adults followed by reflections on the nature and dynamics of caring pedagogy in the classroom. These areas have far reaching consequences for the classroom and form the foundation for caring pedagogy.

BACKGROUND: THE CONTEXT PROVIDED BY THE 1980S

There were profound shifts in thinking about education and educational practices in the 1980s that gave major impetus to the focus on care and caring pedagogy. Fueled by the public policy initiatives to reform public education and the accompanying attention directed at teachers, a few education scholars helped us rethink the qualities of teaching and learning.

The scholarship of Nel Noddings at Stanford University in her pioneering work on care (1984), created a wake in the deep waters of traditional analytic philosophy and behavioral psychology of learning. She helped unsettle the quietly complacent waters of the objectivist traditions and stimulated imaginative work among scholars in education who, in the late 1980s, started to focus more on the qualities of connected relationships between teachers and students. Noddings' work was supported by the similar voice of Carol Gilligan at Harvard University who challenged the traditional, positivist, hierarchical, male approach to moral development. Gilligan (1982) focused on a connected and caring construction of moral choices.

The work of these and other feminist scholars was complemented by other scholars writing in the genre of aesthetics education and qualitative ways of knowing. Eisner, for example, focused on the imagination (1985) and the enlightened eye (1991) in which he observes that:

> Both the content of the world and the content of our imagination are dependent upon qualities. It is through the perception of qualities—not only those we can see, but those we experience through any of our senses—that our consciousness comes into being. (An enlightened eye perceives qualities) that pervade intimate social relations and those that constitute complex social institutions, such as schools. (p. 1)

The other side of the coin in perceiving, Eisner notes, is communicating the content of our consciousness. It involves giving public form to that content and sharing our experience so that another may know it in a meaningful way. Although Eisner does not specifically focus on the issue of care, his work, along with Greene (1995) and others, has helped open the conversation about curriculum and the arts and stimulated a deeper analysis of relational or connected knowing.

In addition to the work of feminist scholars, such as Noddings and Gilligan, and curriculum theorists focusing on the arts, such as Eisner and Greene, critical theorists such as Giroux (1992) and Apple (1996) were providing unsettling analyses of the culture and politics of education. New philosophies and methods of inquiry were emerging as paradigmatic critiques were raising fundamental epistemological questions about the positivist assumptions of most research informing educational practice. These challenges to the established cannons of research, curriculum, and teaching created powerful debates with vast possibilities for new understandings. Among these was the focus on the existential experience of students in caring relationships with teachers.

Although deeply rooted in the humanities with applications in humanistic education and psychology, the articulation of an ethic of care in the mid 1980s took on new meaning. Rather than part of a devalued "soft" rhetoric (in contrast to the valued "hard" science of education), the discussion of care and transformative qualities of caring relationships was perceived to have meaningful implications for the core debates about school reform and what is important in the classroom.

Much of the debate about school reform has turned, and continues to turn, on the issue of objective outcome accountability—an inevitable issue that must be accommodated (Eisner, 1998). Caring pedagogy has outcomes. A caring relationship with a teacher has consequences that are different from a detached or cruel relationship. What students experience and the emotional memories they take with them for the rest of their lives affect their attitudes toward themselves and others.

More attention is being directed to what goes on in the classroom to produce those outcomes. However, even more attention remains focused on what the quantitative outcomes of teaching should be than on the kinds of experiences that children need to have in the classroom.

A major concern now is how do we understand the lived experience in the classroom in ways that respect, honor, and promote growth in the moral, spiritual, and intellectual lives of children and their teachers? The conversation about teaching and learning cannot return to the comfortable mooring of objective science. The tangles of what we know and how we know it, of who we are and how we learn, of the occasions for and products of experience, are too tight. Neither scientific methods that reject subjectivity nor political rhetoric that advocates separating "basics" from the rest of what must be experienced and learned in school will untangle the moral and epistemological threads that now form the complex, and sometimes incoherent, discourses on teaching and learning.

Major shifts in moral and philosophical perspectives and culture during the past two decades have impacted educational scholarship and have contributed to the growth of interest in caring pedagogy. Postmodern scholarship and a reawakened interest in Deweyan pragmatism have helped focus attention on the nature of the self and its relationships, whether with other selves or with curricula, that create the opportunities for experience. The traditional divisions—self and other, mind and matter, observer and observed, teaching and learning, knowledge and knowing, and teacher and student—are disappearing and being replaced by conceptions of multiple selves and multiple realities. The divisions, so deeply entrenched in the positivist tradition, never worked for Dewey in his view of students and their learning. Now the challenges of postmodern scholars include both/and rather than either/or thinking, simultaneous realities, chaos, and locally constructed and situated knowledge. This revolution in thinking during the past two decades has transformed (or is in the process of transforming) our understandings of mind, thinking, learning, knowledge, inquiry, and self. It is in this context that the pedagogies of care are being examined. Care is being understood as relational and connected in discourses concerned with the nature of self, community, and multiple realities.

MEMORIES OF CARING PEDAGOGY

Abstract discussion aimed at gaining some general understanding of the concept of care runs the risk of missing the existential nature of the experience. Caring and receiving care motivate many gestures. The acts and language used to communicate caring are manifestations of an inner reality of positive regard. Caring is a real personal experience of connection and respect that endures in the memory of those who care and are cared about. Letters to former teachers written by adults who are now teachers provide a window into the nature and qualities of caring. (See Chapter 3 for a discussion of letter writing and memories of noncaring teachers.) In the following section we discuss the lived and remembered experience of caring pedagogy in the classroom. Although there are many themes and dimensions of caring pedagogy, three are discussed here and illustrated with letters that provide remembered accounts of having cared and having been cared for in the classroom. These include hospitality to strangers, safety, and gestures of civility. It is significant to observe that although these themes of caring pedagogy suggest teacher virtues, the memories of profound experiences of being cared for recorded in the letters emphasize the powerful relationship of the teachers and their students.

Hospitality to Strangers

Dear Miss Adams,

My name is Maria Lake. When I met you my name was Naria Jacobellis. I entered your classroom September 30, 1960. I had arrived from Italy a few days earlier. I came with my dad, my cousin who spoke English, and the principal to your door. I felt so small standing there in the middle of these four adults. I couldn't understand the words being spoken but I knew what was being discussed. The principal was telling you that you were going to have me in your class and that I didn't speak any English, I had just arrived from Italy. You listened to your principal and my cousin, shook my dad's hand and then looked down at me with the biggest, friendliest smile that I can still see clearly today. I did understand the word "hi" but mostly I understood your body language. I was immediately comfortable and when my dad handed me over to you, you took me by the shoulders and led me into class. Hands still placed on my shoulders, you introduced me to the class. The children were all staring and I wished I could have shrunk into the floor, but you guided me straight to a friendly smiling face of a girl named "Mary." Was that a coincidence? Perhaps. She was going to be my "buddy" for however long I needed to get to know my way around. Miss Adams, I think of you often and I thank my lucky stars that you were my first experience with education in this new country. I'll never forget how you chose me and little Gary to be in your wedding shower picture that the local paper came to take. I'll never forget how you let me play "Little Red Riding Hood" in the class play even though I had only been in Canada two months. Was I a natural in learning new languages? I think not! I remember how you praised me after the play and explained to the audience of parents how I had only been in Canada two months. I beamed!

Miss Adams, this is a note to thank you for having been so willing and happy to take on what was probably your first ESL student and for accepting me. It later inspired me to go into teaching. I made up my mind sometime during the first grade that I would be a teacher too. And I am!

Thanks,
Maria

This is a record of a relationship, frozen in time in Maria's memory, of Miss Adams, her first grade teacher. Maria remembers her fear and her need for support as a new student who didn't speak English. She remembers the manner in which she was received and welcomed as a stranger by her teacher. Maria has never forgotten Miss Adams's smile, her comforting touch, and the sensitive way she introduced Maria into the classroom filled with strangers. She felt valued and was quickly given a place in the class. Miss Adams's hospitality dissolved Maria's apprehension and helped her connect with the class and the curriculum. Although there are principles of etiquette that may be used in greeting and welcoming strangers, even for first graders who don't speak the language being spoken in the school, it was not just what Miss Adams did that mattered. It was how she did it and the comforting connection she established with Maria in the process. Maria arrived unknown to anyone and knowing no one. She was an object, an "it," to use Buber's term (1970), until she experienced herself as known, connected, and safe. She was transformed from an object to a subject, an I in an I–thou relationship with Miss Adams.

Emily, like Maria, remembered an experience of being welcomed into a classroom and feeling the supportive care of her teacher, Mr. Clinton.

Dear Mr. Clinton,

Thank you for all the help you gave to me in the fourth grade at Haywood Avenue Elementary. The first day of your class was my first at school. I had moved from Bradenton to Bartow and knew no one except family. I came in crying and wouldn't stop all day. You understood being in a new town, a new house, and a new school. These things are difficult for children, especially ones like me who do not adapt well to change. You would sit me in your lap during group reading and rock away while you read us the best stories. You helped me a lot, and even though it took me a few weeks, you stood by me every step of the way. You are a very special person and a good role model for me as a future teacher. I see you sometimes and you still remember me.

I thank you for your love and care and want you to know that I will love you always.

Love,
Emily

P.S. *Tales of a Fourth Grade Nothing,* the book you read first in our class, will always be my favorite.

Mr. Clinton understood the message in the crying and found ways to comfort Emily that she has never forgotten. Remembering him having "stood by [her] every step of the way" is a powerful emotional memory. He essentially took away the pain of feeling like a stranger. Had he viewed her as an immature fourth grader and approached her differently, she might well have suffered considerable negative impact to her sense of worth and value in the class. He approached her on the most basic level of need, her need for safety and a sense of belonging, having a place.

It is interesting that she remembers *Tales of A Fourth Grade Nothing* in the same memory. Emotional memories have content. We don't partition our thoughts and emotional experiences. We have feelings about what we think and our feelings have intellectual content. Our feeling ashamed, embarrassed, or humiliated, for example, includes understandings of what we believe is happening to us and why. This is fundamental to the way children learn and central to several philosophies of education and theories of learning. Caring pedagogy, then, is about the emotional life of the student and, at the same time, the student's understanding of how and why she is being cared about. Both the emotional experience and the understanding are important in helping the student who is cared about make a caring response. Both are important to the quality of relationship or connection we call caring.

A teacher within a caring pedagogy also remembers that at the start of each new school year, all of the students enter as strangers. In order to construct a welcoming and safe environment for all students, the teacher must build a relationship with each student and facilitate the development of relationships between students. By so doing, the teacher promotes a learning community within the classroom. The safe environment created by a learning community provides fertile ground for social, emotional, and academic growth. As students explore the curriculum, they also explore the new relationships they have with the teacher and fellow classmates. Students learn about themselves when they must negotiate relationships with others (Noddings, 1991). They also learn about multiple perspectives and caring for others. The opposite can happen however, if students' experiences in school take place in a context in which positive regard for others is not emphasized. Kohn (1991) states, "At a tender age, children learn not to be tender. A dozen years of schooling often do nothing to promote generosity or a commitment to the welfare of others. To the contrary, students are graduated who think that being smart means looking out for number one" (p. 498).

A caring pedagogy is committed to encouraging the development of the whole student, not just selected parts. Separating the student from interactions with peers separates a student from a part of him/herself. A caring pedagogy recognizes the rich learning opportunities present when students must negotiate problems and relationships with each other. Through avenues such as conflict resolution, problem solving, debate, and dialogue, students learn that they do not "corner the market" in terms of point of view. They learn that a person's point of view dictates how s/he sees a situation and that while s/he may see a situation differently than others, it does not prevent a constructive dialogue. Thus, students with many differences can learn from each other and form a community in which strangers are embraced and welcomed.

Safety

Dear Mrs. Gilday,

I am one of many students who fondly remembers you. I was very fortunate to have you as my fifth grade teacher. In you we saw dignity, respect, and true caring. Your manner was gentle, your time always given freely. Your lessons were interesting and you had a sense of humor. You did not always call on the waving hands or dismiss incorrect answers or embarrass your students. Rather, you coaxed them along, enabling them to succeed.

We were all individuals to you and were treated with respect. A time I will never forget was when you rescued me from embarrassment. I had put a Valentine cookie in David Johnson's desk and did not put a note in it—just my initials. I was painfully shy and had a huge crush on him. He made a big fuss over this mystery cookie and when the whole class was in an uproar when my identity was discovered, you calmly and gently said something to the effect of "how thoughtful and kind"—thereby settling the class and saving me from embarrassment. I never said it then, but thank you—for everything.

Sincerely,
Grace

Grace has general memories of the qualities of respect and caring Mrs. Gilday brought to her classroom. She remembers how it felt to be there. Her memory of putting a Valentine cookie in David Johnson's desk is terrifying, filled with the potential for humiliation for a fifth grader, especially one who was painfully shy. David's action magnified her fear. Her "identity was discovered" and she became the center of attention. She remembers it precisely because Mrs. Gilday removed the terror, made her feel safe, and respected her by finding the right words to say.

She was rescued. Mrs. Gilday's diplomacy as well as her sensitivity to Grace's embarrassment saved the day.

Reading Grace's letter, one gets the feeling that Mrs. Gilday was really present to her class. Her dignity, sense of humor, and giving of herself and time were remembered as the "who" who Mrs. Gilday was. What she did that was remembered was to take charge of the class in a calm and gentle way and turn an incident in which Grace was being shamed into a teachable moment for commenting on social graces—Grace's thoughtfulness and kindness in giving David the cookie.

Noddings (1992) characterizes the student–teacher relationship as an unequal one, one in which teachers have the responsibility to be the main carer. They must be able to take on the student's perspective, recognizing his/her needs. The teacher must then be able to meet those needs in an affirming way while assuring the academic, emotional, and physical safety of all of the students in the class. Sometimes this requires the teacher to evoke what Noblit (1993) refers to as moral authority. Teachers who evoke moral authority do so without authoritarian oppression. Realizing that the unequal nature of the student–teacher relationship necessitates analysis and reflection, the teacher is cognizant of the impact of his/her authority and has the conviction to carry it out in an ethical manner.

A caring teacher also realizes how personal perceptions or biases can affect his/her relationship with students. How we view others greatly affects how we interact with them (Bruner, 1986). Teachers who have a positive view of their students as individuals are more likely to relate to them in a caring way. Prejudicial thinking can endanger positive regard and in turn endanger the feeling of safety a student is extended in the classroom.

Feeling safe is such a deep emotional experience, it can produce feelings of adoration and hero worship. "Falling in love with your teacher" is likely due, at least in part, to the feeling of complete safety and the sense that you are loved by your teacher. Cicely adored Mrs. Gilbert:

Dear Mrs. Gilbert,

I remember you. I was the little girl in your second grade class at Theodore Roosevelt who smiled all day for the entire year I was in your class. I loved you and everything about being in your class! I can remember so vividly coming up to the Dick and Jane reading circle. I had such a hard time keeping my place when the other boys and girls read. Mostly this was because I couldn't take my eyes off of you. But even when I did lose my place and it was my turn to read, you'd help me along until I finally found the right spot.

I decided that very year that I wanted to grow up to become a teacher just like you. I never forgot you or my dream to become a teacher. I've had some wonderful teachers since I left 2nd grade and I've had some not so wonderful teachers, but you—you were my hero and model when I was barely seven years old.

To this very day, when my little students come up for their daily hug, I can feel your arms around me, making me feel that this place called school was truly a safe and wonderful place to be. My own students now are the benefactors of your very caring ways.

Wherever you are, Mrs. Gilbert, may God bless you always.

Love,

Cicely Walker Thomas

Each of us can probably identify with Cicely's romance with her teacher—"I couldn't take my eyes off of you." As a second grader, Cicely was open to joy and vulnerable to hurt. She sensed that Mrs. Gilbert was a trustworthy person who cared about her. Cicely's own self-love was reflected in what she sensed in Mrs. Gilbert.

Some people exude warmth, trustworthiness, and care. Some don't. We prefer to be with those who do and are much more likely to connect with them in a meaningful way because we don't feel a need to invest so much energy in protecting ourselves. A caring pedagogy is not limited to teachers who have a particular personality or style of relating to children. However, gentleness and warmth are helpful.

Gestures of Civility

Dear Mrs. Smith,

This letter is to thank you for your kindness and support when I was in your second grade class. If you remember, my father had had a heart attack and was unable to work at that time. My family was receiving public assistance and people were always coming to the school to check my shoes or my coat to see if I qualified for new ones. We stood in line at Christmas to receive one toy and a food basket and it was a humiliating experience for my whole family. You never drew attention to me when I needed to go into the hall to see one of the public assistance workers and you were always adding little things to my lunches. You even did a lesson about having real wealth and I knew that you were talking to me. You were a wonderful, caring teacher and I will never forget you.

THANK YOU!

Jenny

Jenny remembers Mrs. Smith as the teacher who saw beyond her poverty and protected her from humiliation. Mrs. Smith was not only thoughtful and understanding of Jenny's circumstances—perhaps Mrs. Smith had, herself, experienced poverty as a child and felt Jenny's embarrassment—she was able to translate her sensitivity into her lesson plans. The moral and political dimensions of the social ecology of the classroom are powerful. A teacher focusing only on instructional objectives or on methods is likely to miss what children are experiencing. Although no one can observe a child's experience, a sensitive teacher is likely to know her students' personal stories and to be able to interpret different meanings of what is said and done that might not be noticed by an observer. In this respect, the sensitive teacher sees more than is apparent and hears more than what is said. She reads the silences, the interaction patterns, the stares, the facial display patterns, and other behavior with social meaning. A sensitive teacher is empathic and her caring motivates her own actions to connect with students, to anticipate and prevent unkindness, and to be present when and as needed to her students. The teacher's moral vision and care inspire the pedagogy of the classroom for students as well as objective considerations of the formal curriculum. Mrs. Smith knew Jenny and cared enough about her experience in the classroom to engineer activities to protect Jenny's privacy and integrity.

Mrs. Chapel was also remembered as a teacher who knew the graces of thoughtfulness and care.

Dear Mrs. Chapel,

You were my fourth grade teacher. You made learning a way of life! When we talked about Indians, we made Indians, Indian homes, Indian food. No matter who made it, you showed us how wonderful it was through their eyes. I remember being made fun of because I had really thick glasses and red hair. You explained how "four eyes" was an Indian Chief (wise because of his four eyes) who found a young girl with red hair like "fire" and she became an Indian Princes. You helped me through other sad times in my life by looking at it from a different viewpoint.

When you came back from Christmas holiday you brought us all a piece of maple candy in the shape of a maple leaf. You brought us maple leaves and we made a maple tree and learned about the maple tree and how it related to Indians and the "New America."

At science project time, you helped me find a book on seashells. As a gift for a winning science project you had a set of "boxed" shells sent out to my home. I had never received any mail until that time in my life.

You made me feel very special and worthwhile. You told my mother I was really going to be somebody someday.

Thank you,
Billy

Billy has specific memories of Mrs. Chapel as a good teacher who helped him find the right book for his project and who made learning a way of life. He also remembers her acts of kindness in destigmatizing his appearance, bringing treats to school, and making positive comments to his mother. He sums up his memory of Mrs. Chapel: "You made me feel very special and worthwhile." He remembers feeling cared for and, as evidenced in his letter of her unforgotten graces, he continues to care for her.

What Billy remembers is his relationship with Mrs. Chapel; what she did and what he experienced. An educational anthropologist would not have been able to observe the meaning her assistance with the book would have or the lasting impression she made in giving dignity to the term "four eyes." That which an observer may never have seen, and likely would not have been able to report, Billy has never forgotten. The fun, food, assistance, and respect all form different textures in a single fabric, a memory of Mrs. Chapel and her caring pedagogy in the classroom.

Each of us examine these letters in different ways and likely find different meanings in them. Each situation described has a context about which we know little or nothing. We don't know the teacher or the student writing the letter. What we do know is that the student had an experience that he or she has not forgotten. When asked to remember a caring teacher, Maria, Jenny, and Billy quickly recovered these beautiful stories in which they felt cared about by a caring teacher. They remember the pedagogy as nurture, safety, and respect. They may or may not remember the capital of France or when World War I ended, but they remember these caring teachers who made them feel special. They have carried this pedagogy in their hearts into their lives as adults.

CARING ABOUT THE CURRICULUM AND EDUCATIONAL GOALS

The concept of caring pedagogy carries meaning that includes and extends beyond the general understanding of care in our society. Care is usually taken to be synonymous with nurture, affection, and support and it suggests an attitude as well as behavior. Caring parents want their children to develop the understandings, attitudes, and skills needed to succeed in life. Therefore, they attempt to meet, or make arrangements so that others can meet, their children's emotional, physical, and spiritual needs. A basketball coach who cares about his players also wants them to win games and prepares them for competition. A caring teacher wants her students to learn the subjects she teaches and takes responsibility for planning and implementing a curriculum that reflects her care. Her relationship with students is not limited to nurture; it extends to caring about her students learning and succeeding. Caring pedagogy, then, includes the teacher's motivation and preparedness to teach as well as her disposition of positive regard for her students. The ethic of care in teaching, we believe, implies competence as a responsible manifestation of caring.

We agree with Noddings that while teaching students to be caring and responsible citizens is a higher goal than teaching academic subjects, the choice is not necessary. We do recognize, however, that a teacher who nurtures and maintains a caring relationship with students can, at the same time, fail to address instructional objectives. This is dramatically illustrated in the following letter to Mr. Harden.

Dear Mr. Carson,

You were my sixth grade teacher. At the time, I thought you were the best teacher I had ever had. All of the students in the class adored you and it seemed like you cared for us also. You exposed us to the world of art and encouraged us to "create" in the classroom's art center. You let us have "our space" when we needed it by giving us a hall pass when we wanted to take a walk around the school campus. We were also given a lot of time throughout the day to read in the reading corner and get into groups with classmates and discuss anything we wanted to. I learned a lot about forming relationships with peers during that time. The main thing I remember about your class is that we had a lot of fun. We did not spend much time learning new concepts in math, science, or social studies or about composing our thoughts and putting them on paper. But, it didn't seem to matter at the time. We were all enjoying the moment and the freedom you afforded us.

I must tell you however, the next year in seventh grade, I found myself struggling to keep up academically with my peers. School policy at that time utilized a tracking system that separated students into achievement groups based on standardized test scores taken at the end of sixth grade. I was placed in one of the lower tracks based on my scores as were other students who had been in your class. I began to doubt my intellectual abilities and this self-doubt was reinforced as I struggled through my classes. It took me quite some time to recover academically and have faith in my intellectual abilities. I often wonder if my path would have been different had I not experienced such self-doubt and struggle.

You seemed like such a caring person, but possibly you did not realize that when caring for a student you must consider the whole student and his/her potential. Creating a climate of care in the classroom must also extend into the realm of facilitating the intellectual and academic growth of students. It seems to me that caring environment should never be limiting; instead they should offer possibilities and affirmation to the mind, the heart, and the soul.

Your former student,
Allison

Mr. Carson provided an emotionally safe and welcoming environment but failed to nurture Karen's intellectual development. Just as harm can be induced by the absence of emotional nurturance, harm can also be inflicted through the lost realization of intellectual potential.

FACILITATING RELATIONSHIPS BETWEEN STUDENTS AND THE CURRICULUM

Caring teachers are not only cognizant of the relationships they form with students, they are equally cognizant of the relationships they must facilitate between the students and the curriculum. Caring relationships offer genuine connection through a realm of possibilities. The lack of connection often provides limits and roadblocks. It has been reported in the literature that students often feel a disconnection in terms of school and what is taught there (Noddings, 1992; Poplin & Weeres, 1992; Raffini, 1993). Traditionally, the curriculum within schools has been viewed as a body of knowledge (developed by experts) that is to be learned by students. When knowledge is seen as existing outside of the individual (in the curriculum), it restricts the ways in which a student can interact with/relate to the curriculum and disconnection occurs. What typically results is that a student's interaction/relationship with the curriculum is one-dimensional and often superficial. They "learn" (remember) information in the curriculum long enough to perform on tests but are not able to apply or generalize the information in any meaningful way (Brandt, 1993). The information, not being meaningful to the student, becomes a wedge between the student and school and can contribute to the student's disconnection and alienation.

Within a caring pedagogy the teacher carefully cultivates a relationship between the students and the curriculum. The curriculum is not seen as a string of related facts to be memorized by the student but rather areas of information to be explored, critiqued, and analyzed.

> Children naturally try to make sense of the world—to figure out how magnets work or why friends help. Good teaching fosters these efforts to understand, but also hones them, helping children become ever more skillful, reflective, and self-critical in their pursuit of knowledge. (Lewis, Schaps, & Watson, 1996, p. 18)

As facilitators, teachers within a caring pedagogy think about many areas when cultivating a positive relationship between their students and the curriculum. These areas include but are not limited to connections, engagement, difference, and metacognition.

Connections

All students have experiences and understandings through which they filter the world and construct knowledge (Ellsworth, 1989). A caring pedagogy affirms the student by affirming what s/he brings to the classroom. By giving voice and importance to what the students know, a teacher can show students how they are connected to the curriculum. By connecting new ideas and concepts to ones that already exist for the student, the new ideas/concepts become grounded and new knowledge can be constructed. An example would be the use of metaphors, such as using the metaphor of family to explore the roles and relationships of individuals in organizations. Metaphors awaken meaning based on images, understandings, and even stories within our schemas. This type of personal meaning is very powerful and can transcend language (Horton & Freire, 1990). As the student makes meaning out of the new concepts or ideas, they are not simply added to the schema but rather transform the schema and new knowledge is constructed (Poplin, 1988).

Addressing the social issues and real life concerns that the students face also provides important connections between the student and the curriculum. Issues such as violence in the community could be explored through data gathering, leading to generated solutions that could be tested. This type of connection helps students see that school is a part of their world and their life rather than a disconnected entity. Students become invested in exploring and solving problems that are of concern to them and their community. As Newman and Wehlage (1993) state,

> They explore these connections in ways that create personal meaning. Students are involved in an effort to influence an audience beyond their classroom; for example, by communicating knowledge to others, advocating solutions to social problems, providing assistance to people, or creating performances or products with utilitarian or aesthetic value. (p. 10).

By moving beyond the classroom and expanding the students' view of community to include all of humanity, a caring teacher can connect student learning to issues of social justice. Students learn about responsible citizenship through actively confronting issues such as injustice and racism. Connecting students to the world community provides a context in which all of the subject areas of the curriculum can be explored. Not only is intellect developed and nurtured through the process but also the students' sense of humanity and self.

Engagement

Passivity breeds apathy and disconnection. When students are passively rather than actively involved in learning, the relationship between students and the curriculum is jeopardized. On the other hand, passionate engagement of the student with the curriculum can provide unlimited possibilities. The arousal of curiosity and the encouragement of creativity can engage the student's mind as well as his/her heart. A curriculum that leaves room for the student to wonder and wander provides fertile ground for curiosity and creativity. A teacher who recognizes a student's need to make choices and explore possibilities facilitates that student's relationship with the curriculum. Passionate engagement can be fostered in many ways, such as discussions and debates with other students about multiple perspectives on events and ideas, presentation of concepts and ideas in new and even contradictory contexts, and encouraging new ways of knowing and understanding.

Related to engagement is motivation. Within a caring pedagogy, students are empowered by teachers who see that the most productive type of motivation is internal rather than external. Coercing engagement through external motivators is based on control rather than authentic engagement (Kohn, 1996). Teachers often see control as an effective means to stave off chaos. But, as Kohn (1996) states:

> Counterpoising control to chaos . . . has the effect of ruling out any other possibilities. But this isn't an error in logic so much as it is a statement about one's view of the people in the classroom. It says that students—or perhaps humans in general—must be tightly regulated if they are to do anything productive. Notice that this doesn't merely speak to the value of having some *structure* to their activities; it says that external *control* is necessary, and without it, students are unlikely to learn or to act decently. (p. 2)

Instructional environments that are controlling and rigid in their focus limit a student's ability to construct meaning and may even limit the neural connections in the brain through "neural pruning" (Cardellichio & Field, 1997). A caring pedagogy is about possibilities rather than limits and absolute control. A classroom in which the students are authentically engaged in the curriculum is not chaotic but lively, thought provoking, constantly changing, and satisfying. The teacher is comfortable with the students' high level of engagement because he/she is thoughtfully orchestrating and facilitating the process. The teacher and the students become partners in learning; partners in possibilities.

Difference

Students come to school with many differences. Some are visible, such as physical differences, and some are not, such as the way students learn or process information. Teachers who do not have a positive regard for students, their differences, and their capabilities, limit student learning, either consciously or subconsciously (Horton & Freire, 1990; Kozol, 1991). Within a caring pedagogy however, access to learning is not earned through compliance, awarded as a result of previous achievement, or granted on the basis of social, economic, or cultural background; it simply exists for all. Teachers within a caring pedagogy see differences not as deficiencies but as characteristics of the individual. The teacher is also aware that each student's relationship with the curriculum and learning is influenced by those characteristics. Therefore, just as each student is unique, each student's relationship with the curriculum is also unique.

When thinking about curriculum and instruction, some teachers believe they are being fair when they argue that every student should receive the same materials, same instruction, and engage in the same interactions as everyone else. However, fairness has less to do with sameness than it does with need. When every student gets what s/he needs in terms of materials, instruction, and interaction, then fairness prevails. For instance, some students may have difficulty processing visual information presented on an overhead projector. A teacher within a caring pedagogy would recognize this difference and provide the student with alternate materials or provide opportunities for verbal discussion with peers about the information. By recognizing differences and accommodating those differences, students are affirmed in their unique way of learning and constructing knowledge. When a good "fit" or relationship is established between the student and the curriculum, sameness becomes a moot point.

Difference within the curriculum itself must also be considered. Students become limited in their ability to understand events, issues, and concepts if they are immersed in a curriculum that is too narrow in its point of view. A curriculum that embraces multiple perspectives provides more possibilities for deeper understandings. By looking at issues, events, and concepts from different perspectives, the student also becomes aware of the presence of multiple voices; voices that are not "right" or "wrong," but rather different points of view that provide a more complete picture. The affirmation of multiple voices within the classroom provides the students with a safe environment in which to contemplate, debate, address misconceptions, and develop new ways of thinking.

Metacognition

A student's positive relationship with the curriculum, as with any relationship, entails responsibility. Metacognition helps one to have some awareness of his/her own learning process and to have some measure of control over it. Metacognition reinforces the notion that there are different ways of thinking and knowing. Billingsley and Wildman (1990) point out that most definitions of metacognition consider two main areas: metacognitive knowledge and self-regulation. Metacognitive knowledge is an understanding about how we approach learning and how we learn best. Self-regulation has to do with our internal assessment of understanding as we approach information.

When teachers encourage students to explore their own learning and construct metacognitive knowledge, they facilitate the development of independent learners. If students know what strategies and processes are most productive for them in approaching new information, they will be less dependent on others to help them make meaning from information and, therefore, will be less limited in the learning process.

In order to facilitate the development of metacognitive knowledge, teachers must be open to letting students explore different strategies and methods when approaching information and problems rather than insist on rigid procedures, algorithms, and so on. Students learn how they process information by making choices and examining those choices within the process they followed. They begin to recognize what works best for them.

Students also need to develop self-regulation by being cognizant of when they have constructed meaning from information and when they have not. Teachers who encourage students to explain their reasoning, discuss their understandings, and pinpoint misconceptions facilitate self-regulation. When a student realizes that s/he does not understand encountered information, then s/he may try personal strategies or processes (from their metacognitive knowledge) such as using reference materials, drawing an illustration, using visual imagery, or asking for help. Students come to realize that the constructing of knowledge is not relegated to others but is within them. This empowerment can translate into a love of learning that extends beyond the school year and transcends the classroom.

CONCLUSION

Care in the classroom involves, among other things, the one caring and the response of the one cared about (Noddings, 1992). It is an experience of positive regard that may occur in moments, may be episodic, or may be enduring. "Caring is a way of being in relation(ships), not a set of specific behaviors" (p. 17).

We believe caring pedagogy involves meaningful and authentic relationships between teachers and students that nurture growth and facilitate learning. It is "being there" together, regarding the other as present and deserving respect in a way that transforms both, much as Buber (1970) described in an I–thou relationship. For Buber I–thou was one word, it was a relationship that joined, supplanting the I–it relationship that objectified, depersonalized, and distanced the other in ways that required no particular moral regard.

A caring pedagogy cannot be dictated or coerced. It must be the product of a genuine concern regarding the needs of students. Students are allowed to flourish in their own way within a caring pedagogy and teachers are comfortable in acting as facilitators within that process. Teachers are also aware of the critical role they play in the relationships formed within schools. They critically evaluate their professional practice and carefully analyze the impact their actions and decisions have on students. Teachers within a caring pedagogy also act as advocates for students when they encounter systems that jeopardize students' emotional, academic, and physical safety.

The contrast between a caring pedagogy and a negative pedagogy is not always clear. Rather, it is often the difference between an awareness of the ethical nature of teaching and a sensitivity to the impact a teacher can have in the life of a child, and the absence of that awareness/sensitivity. Within a negative pedagogy, teachers may have a positive regard for students and wish to do them no harm. However, due to their lack of sensitivity to ethical issues such as the impact of their actions and decisions on students, harm is inflicted. A caring pedagogy encourages careful and critical examination of practices/policies, philosophies, and actions. When mistakes are made, they are owned, analyzed, and "made right" with the students when possible. Tough ethical decisions, such as carrying out actions that may be perceived as hurtful to some in order to be helpful to others (i.e., no-tolerance policies), are not taken lightly, but carefully thought out and discussed with those they impact.

Schools and classrooms exist within complex systems that can seem bureau-cratic and uncaring. A caring pedagogy can help ensure that students do not become "lost" within the system. It provides a context in which a student's educational experiences can become personal, enriching, and affirming.

REFERENCES

Apple, M. (1996). *Cultural politics and education.* New York: Teacher's College Press.

Billingsley, B., & Wildman, T. (1990). Facilitating reading comprehension in learning disabled students: Metacogntitive goals and instructional strategies. *Remedial and Special Education, 11*(2), 18–31.

Brandt, R. (1993). On teaching for understanding: A conversation with Howard Gardner. *Educational Leadership, 50*(7), 4–7.

Bruner, J. (1986). *Actual minds, possible worlds.* Cambridge: Harvard University Press.

Buber, M. (1970). *I and thou.* New York: Touchstone.

Cardellichio, T., & Field, W. (1997). Seven strategies that encourage neural branching. *Educational Leadership 54*(6), 33–36.

Eisner, E. (1979). *The educational imagination: On the design and evaluation of school programs.* New York: Macmillan.

Eisner, E. (1985). *The educational imagination: On the design and evaluation of school programs.* New York: Macmillan.

Eisner, E. (1998). The enlightened eye: Qualitative inquiry and the enhancement of educational practice. Columbus, OH: Merrill.

Ellsworth, E. (1989). Why doesn't this feel empowering? Working through the repressive myths of critical pedagogy. *Harvard Educational Review, 59,* 297–324.

Gilligan, C. (1982). *In a different voice.* Cambridge: Harvard University Press.

Giroux, H. (1992). *Border crossings: Cultural workers and the politics of education.* New York: Routledge.

Greene, M. (1995). Releasing the imagination: Essays on education, the arts, and social change. San Francisco: Jossey-Bass.

Horton, M., & Freire, P. (1991). *We make the road by walking: Conversations on education and social change.* Philadelphia: Temple University Press.

Kohn, A. (1991). Caring kids: The role of the schools. *Phi Delta Kappan, 72*(7), 496–506.

Kohn, A. (1993). *Beyond discipline: From compliance to community.* Alexandria, VA: Association for Supervision and Curriculum Development.

Kozol, J. (1991). *Savage inequalities: Children in America's schools.* New York: Holt, Rinehart & Winston.

Lewis, C., Schaps, E., & Watson, M. (1996). The caring classroom's academic edge. *Educational Leadership, 54*(1), 16–21.

Newman, F., & Wehlage, G. (1993). Five standards of authentic instruction. *Educational Leadership,* April, 8–12.

Noblit, G. (1993). Power and caring. *American Educational Research Journal, 30*(1), 23–38.

Noddings, N. (1984). *Caring: A feminine approach to ethics and moral education.* Berkeley: University of California Press.

Noddings, N. (1991). Stories in dialogue: Caring and interpersonal relationships. In C. Witherell & N. Noddings (Eds.), *Stories lives tell: Narrative and dialogue in education*, pp. 157–171. New York: Teacher's College Press.

Noddings, N. (1992). *The challenge to care in schools: An alternative approach to education.* New York: Teachers College Press.

Poplin, M. S. (1988). Holistic/constructivist principles of the teaching/learning process: Implications for the filed of learning disabilities. *Journal of Learning Disabilities, 21*(7), 401–416.

Poplin, M., & Weeres, J. (1992). *Voices from the inside: A report on schooling from inside the classroom.* Claremont, CA: Institute for Education in Transformation.

Raffini, J. (1993). *Winners without losers: Structures and strategies for increasing student motivation to learn.* Boston, MA: Allyn and Bacon.

5

CULTURAL CONSTRUCTIONS OF LIFE AND MEANING IN THE CLASSROOM

Yolanda G. Martinez
Orange County Health Department, Florida

Terry Jo Smith
National-Louis University

In the previous two chapters, pedagogy was explored through the lenses of care and cruelty. In this chapter, education is framed as a cultural experience filtered through a diversity of perceptions. The same classroom practice, from a multicultural perspective, may be experienced as caring by some students and cruel by others. In truth, all students suffer in classrooms and schools which do not honor and celebrate diversity. Students learn, as Colucci pointed out in Chapter 3, both the formal and informal curriculum. Classrooms that privilege mainstream culture and denigrate, ignore, or silence other cultural views teach this to children by example. The children whose culture is privileged are deprived of the richness of multiple perspectives and are given a false sense of their own supremacy, while those children whose cultures are not honored or are dishonored experience humiliation and pain. The writer of the following letter expresses the pain of being dishonored.

Dear Mr. J.,

You would have remembered me as one of the three grade eight students who you separated in your 8th grade science class because we came from Bridgeview. I remember the first day of junior high school, how humiliating! What a whirlwind of newness, strangeness and noise. There were only seven of us, a tight knit group of kids from the wrong side of the tracks—terrified of all the others but secretly hopeful that we would be accepted. We entered your classroom with a relief that at least in this block we had 3 of us and we sat down at the science table together. We were quiet, too intimidated by the lab and sparkling science equipment to say anything. We were not causing any trouble. I had always been a good science student, I loved the subject and was looking forward to grade 8 science. My past teachers had helped me recognize that I was a gifted student and I saw grade 8 science as a way to broaden my science experiences. I looked forward to your classes in anticipation. When you started the class by calling the roll, I was surprised when you appeared to stumble over my name. My surprise turned to anxiety and then fear, when you hesitated over Jerry and Mark's name too! Horror took over when you called out to the class that the three kids from Bridgeview move to the back of the room. You can't do this! I thought to myself but I numbly stumbled to the back to await your explanation. As you walked toward us you said that we couldn't do the grade 8 work because our old school didn't have the right equipment. "You guys couldn't do grade 8 science." We already knew we were different! It was reinforced into every facet of our being. Every person that we dealt with in that school, indicated that we were different in some way or another! Did you know that you gave other kids license to treat us differently? Do you know that end of the day I got beaten up and others were locked up in lockers?

I vowed then to never let anyone treat me like that again. Of course, that never really happened and it happened time and time again. But I know that I will never and have never, separated and isolated students because of who they are and where they come from.

This memory did not surface for 20 years—perhaps because the teacher committed suicide at the end of this term and I felt that I could not be critical.

S. L.

INTRODUCTION

The words used by the author of this letter to describe his experience in a new school are powerful. He describes his feelings as a "whirlwind" of "newness" and "strangeness." He reveals his vulnerability as he describes his inner feelings as "secretly hopeful," yet his encounter with this teacher left him feeling intimidated and humiliated. Sadly, this student's experiences aren't unique or even rare. Education in the United States has a long history of inequitable treatment in relation to students who do not belong to mainstream culture. Several cultural theorists (Giroux, 1983; Kohl, 1994; MacLeod, 1995; McLaren, 1985) have concluded that culturally diverse students often experience assaults on their cultural identities in schools which cause them so much pain that some may resist education altogether in order to maintain their personal integrity. Kohl (1994) calls this phenomenon "not-learning" and describes difficult choices that students often face within oppressive educational contexts.

> Not-learning tends to take place when someone has to deal with unavoidable challenges to her or his personal and family loyalties, integrity, and identity. In such situations there are forced choices and no apparent middle ground. To agree to learn from a stranger who does not respect your integrity causes a major loss of self. The only alternative is to not-learn and reject the stranger's world. (p. 20)

Often teachers are unaware, from their position of privilege, of the pain a white, middle-class education causes students of color and/or the working class. This is one of the failures of their own monocultural education. Kohl (1994) describes a recognition of his own cultural insensitivity before meeting a student who was brave enough to challenge his views.

> Before knowing him, I was not attuned to many of the nuances of racist implication because I was not a victim of racism. I did not suffer through every offensive phrase I encountered when reading, nor did I experience rage when racism was cloaked in the authority of tradition or the language of excellence. The lack of that sensitivity bothered me, and I had to unlearn this insensitivity to biased yet traditional ways of speaking and writing. In addition, I had to learn how to choose my own language and learn to make the avoidance of racist reference habit. . . . I had to learn to think from the perspective of someone who had not-learned racist language, and that experience has been an important part of my growth and development. (p. 20)

Teachers are rarely taught in their teacher education programs that they may need to learn to think differently in order to be caring teachers for all students. Multicultural education is often presented in superficial ways, as involving the celebration of holidays and the exploration of ethnic foods. While these types of activities are not to be discounted, when they occur within a white supremacist mindset, they often lack the vitality to transform consciousness.

In this chapter we first take a quick historical glance at education in the United States in relationship to diverse students. This is a sobering story that helps sensitize us to the legacy of cruel practices that have occurred in the name of education when viewed from non-mainstream perspectives. Next, we look at theoretical perspectives that attempt to explain differences in educational attainment for diverse students. Even some of these theoretical perspectives, which undergird intervention strategies, maintain a white supremacist stance. In particular, we focus on theories of social and cultural capital. After examining some of the historical, social, and theoretical foundations of educational practice, we focus on teacher education and pedagogical stances that offer hopeful directions toward creating educational systems that honor all students.

HISTORICAL ROOTS

U.S. schools, as we know them today, developed during the 19th century with some basic guiding principles. According to Stout (1993, p. 301) schools were developed to:

- serve all children equally (except the children of the slaves and other excluded children);
- be supported by public tax dollars rather than by private means;
- teach Americanism in a value-rich, although secular environment;
- be as inexpensive as possible, governed by citizens in decentralized jurisdictions, and given very broad and significant responsibilities.

These principles are some of the seeds from which our current educational practices have sprung. Deeply embedded in the soil of U.S. history we see the roots of oppressive practices toward people of color, which are sometimes difficult to excavate as they are grounded in U.S. traditions.

Traditionally, those who have occupied subordinate positions have not been able to influence policy effectively. Native Americans comprise one of the groups historically relegated to a subordinate position. Although educational policies directed at Native American children have changed dramatically, the primary objective of initial legislation was to Americanize. The boarding school system created in the 19th century had as its primary objective to "kill the Indian but save the man" (Lesiak & Jones, 1991). During this period in American history, Native American children were separated from their families to help them with the process of change. Upon their arrival to the boarding schools, children's physical appearances were immediately changed. Their traditional clothing was taken away and replaced by Western clothing and, in the case of boys, their hair was cut short. This was considered the beginning of the transformation. Forced to sleep on the floor on cold winter nights with a bare blanket to cover their frozen, malnourished bodies, children died of maltreatment and sadness. A policy of extermination had later become one of relocation and finally one of assimilation in post–Civil War years.

In pre–Civil War America, educating African slaves was considered unnecessary given the tasks they were designated to perform in the mines, or in the sugarcane and cotton fields. The post–Civil War Reconstruction brought a period of relative progress and physical liberation for African slaves. In the South, however, Jim Crow laws continued to marginalize and segregate African Americans, limiting their access to education, among other things. In the South, African

Americans were subject to an overt racist mentality; in the North, however, pressure was brought on by industrialists who had helped establish schools for former slaves and hoped that upon graduation they would help increase the productivity in the manufacturing companies. During the 1960s, the notion of "separate but equal" generated a tremendous amount of social discontent, and has, over the years, created numerous issues.

Some immigrant groups have faced some of the same discrimination and marginalization that Native Americans and African Americans have encountered over the years. Only two hundred years ago, students who did not speak English (only those from European language groups) were afforded education in their native language, whereas today the ability to speak another language is perceived as a deficiency. When one looks at the fierce political struggles surrounding bilingual education, it also becomes apparent that the ability to speak another language is also perceived as a threat. Should the United States be a bilingual nation or not? Should the Constitution recognize English as its official language and, as a result, curtail or eliminate federal programs that provide assistance to non–English-speaking individuals? Is the concern that the United States will undergo a linguistic coup d'etat as that experienced by Quebec?

There is also a group of children who, while sharing some of the characteristics mentioned above, are at an educational disadvantage for another reason: mobility. The children of migrant and seasonal farm workers are usually the most profoundly affected by the migratory nature of their parents' subsistence method (Martinez, 1994). The essential characteristics that differentiate migrant students from the rest of the school-age population is mobility. Some aspects associated with the school performance of migrant children include: adjustment problems, gaps in their education, discrimination, lack of community support, and limited parental involvement in the education of their children.

Migrant students are also at the mercy of the system. In many cases, systemic policies impede the educational advancement of migrant students. Some issues include poor identification, lack of credit exchange between educational agencies, and rigid state and local requirements. Migrant students are eligible for special education services; however, due to their mobility and the lengthy process used to identify and determine special educational services, many migrant students do not graduate from high school.

Some of the historical events that brought to the forefront the needs of children from diverse linguistic backgrounds in the 1960s included the influx of children as a result of the Cuban exodus, the Chicano movement on the West coast, and the Civil Rights movement. Over the years, the educational system has developed into a complex bureaucratic machine. Legislation and litigation have been two primary mechanisms used in efforts to provide equal educational opportunities. In an attempt to alleviate some of the problems faced by disadvantaged children in the schooling process, the federal government has enacted a series of policies to ensure diverse students' equal access to education. The decades of the 1960s and 1970s reflect a marked awareness of the needs of children who had been previously neglected. The Bilingual Education Act, The Indian Education Act, The Education for All Handicapped Children Act (PL 94-142), and Title IX were laws enacted during this period in attempts to protect the rights of children who had been previously ignored. However, a conservative social climate and an indifferent national administration in the 1980s diminished much of the momentum toward social justice sparked in the previous decades. Gay (1993) cites some examples of this backward trend:

- The cutting of more than 750,000 children from Chapter 1 programs (the programs of federal educational assistance for economically deprived children).
- Relaxation of requirements for schools receiving federal funds to comply with antidiscrimination laws.
- New funding arrangements that benefit rural and private schools at the expense of urban and inner-city schools.
- Drastic cuts in bilingual, migrant, Indian, and woman's equity educational funding and programs.

In the 1990s and now, many educators are looking at school-reform history and recognizing that legislation is necessary but not sufficient to ensure equality in educational opportunities for all students. There is a growing understanding that roadblocks to social justice may exist much more in an uncritical awareness of our own cultural lenses than in our explicit policies. White supremacy is deeply embedded not only in national history, but in individual psyches and in worldviews of teachers, administrators, and parents. Delpit (1995) describes a shift in emphasis in reform, from worlds outside to worlds inside:

> We all carry worlds in our heads, and those worlds are decidedly different. We educators set out to teach, but how can we reach the worlds of others when we don't even know they exist? Indeed, many of us don't even realize that our own worlds exist only in our heads and in the cultural institutions we have built to support them.
> . . .
> What should we be doing? The answers, I believe, lie not in a proliferation of new reform programs but in some basic understanding of who we are and how we are connected to and disconnected from one another. (p. xiv–xv)

The shifting focus toward critical self-reflection in educational arenas is hopeful. Who we are and how we make sense of our students cannot help but be informed by our racist history. Although we have touched on some groups whose historical treatment in education in the United States has been blatantly oppressive, the ways in which a teacher might construct a student's identity as inferior based on social and political categories is endless. Looking at educational practices through the perspective of race, gender, sexual orientation, religious heritage, and disability, reveals histories of education as a site of painful discrimination and prejudice for many, many students.

The following letter makes it clear that students are very vulnerable in schools. The space between teacher and student provides fertile ground for the enactment of painful discrimination. Our racist, sexist, and classist history is not behind us, but in us, in the worlds we have inside our heads.

Dear M. S—

I'm sure you don't remember me because I am a female and females in your mind are useless inconveniences that only hinder or interfere with the real work of the world—that of men. Nevertheless, I was a student of yours in 9th grade science class—one that you would consider equally forgettable because I was quiet. That fact that I was a good and hard working student was not worthy of note in your scheme of things. Two things about me however, were worthy of note. The first and perhaps not the most important was my Irish heritage. You seemed to deem this very significant in your frequent recitations in class regarding the worthlessness of the Irish, the blight you saw us causing not only in your classroom and school, but also to your nation. I realize now that much of the disgust in your manner towards me and the shame you made me feel was probably just a game to you—a way to make yourself feel more powerful as well as a way to keep a useless female out of your way. The second thing about me and definitely of the utmost importance in your mind was the fact that not only was I a female and a freshman, but I was well-known and even liked by many of your basketball players. (Since my brother was a senior, I was frequently seen in the company of him and his/my friends—Your "stars." Your varsity line-up would stop in the halls to say hi to me, perhaps in your mind momentarily lose their focus on the game at hand—an unpardonable sin—and somehow in effect do the unthinkable and lose a game. Not only was I a useless inconvenience as a female and a freshman, but I would be around for years to further thwart, hinder, and confuse your varsity line-up.)

The fact that I was naive and unaware of any real or imagined impact on the young men you placed in such high regard was obviously immaterial to you. As a full-grown, very tall and very loud man, you took great pride in demeaning and belittling those students you deemed useless and insignificant. The terror I felt and faced each day walking into your classroom was amusing to you. And the ease with which you could have me stand up and make me cry for all the world to see was to me a very cruel and sadistic act. One that you never even legitimized by acting as if it was important—a mere triviality.

I was afraid—in fact terrorized by your treatment of me and remember very little of the subject you taught—the one thing as a teacher that you were responsible for. I wish that I could say that as an adult I could look back on this experience and put it in the context it deserves—but I can't.

Sincerely,
D.

History is taught in school in the formal curriculum, but in a very real sense, history is enacted in schools in the relationships between teachers and students. The painful history of bigotry in our country has been enacted often in classrooms where students are vulnerable. The power embedded in the teacher's role, the power of adults over children, the relatively isolated nature of classrooms, and the power of the institution over the individual combine to create a space in which social oppression can be passed on in the name of education and often with little fear of reprisal. This classroom space, because it is so very powerful, could also be the site of social transformation. We return to this theme later in this chapter and in the final chapter of this book. Next, we look at the theory that informs our practice. Theory is no more free from the racist, white-supremacist attitudes that have deep roots in American psyches and American history than practice.

THEORETICAL IMPLICATIONS FOR INTERVENTION

The educational attainment of students from diverse backgrounds has occupied the attention of educational researchers, anthropologists, and social scientists for decades (Delgado-Gaitan, 1987a, 1987b; Erickson, 1982; Trueba, 1988a, 1988b). In an attempt to find solutions, various theoretical perspectives have been developed over the years to help explain the educational "problems" faced by these students. Explanations of low educational achievement historically have reflected societal attitudes. Cultural discontinuity theories have sought to explain the school failure of some children by proposing that there are discontinuities between the culture of the child and the culture of the school. The major premise behind this perspective emphasizes that the cultural background of the child does not stress American cultural and educational values. In some instances, students' school failure has been blamed on their intellectual inferiority.

Others have relied on the notion of cultural deprivation and have blamed parents for providing a culturally and educationally impoverished environment for their children (Bereiter & Engelman, 1966; Bowles & Gintis, 1976; Deutsch et al., 1967; Hess & Shipman, 1965; Rosenthal & Jacobson, 1968; Sexton, 1961). Opponents of the cultural deprivation theory suggest that children from diverse backgrounds do poorly in school, not because they are culturally deprived, but because they have a culturally different learning environment, that is, they share different cultural domains that influence communication styles, social interaction, and so on. Other explanations have looked at teacher-perceived biases, limited English proficiency, low self-esteem, immigrants' and other groups' perception of their social position in American society, and lack of role models or mentoring opportunities, among other things (Ogbu, 1992, 1995; Teachman, 1987).

John Ogbu attributes outcomes of schooling not only to sociocultural circumstances but to psychological adaptations to American society. Ogbu (1982) agrees with the notion of a cultural difference model, but he suggests that the differences or discontinuities occur at different levels. According to Ogbu, cultural disconti-nuities can be universal (experienced by every school child regardless of culture or economic status), primary (found in those who develop in non-Western settings and emigrate to the United States), and secondary (developed by those who belong to caste-like groups in the United States).

Universal cultural discontinuities are the result of the cultural differences between the home and the school as an institution (socioemotional). For exam-ple, Ogbu suggests that the learning environment at home is informal, inti-mate, interpersonal, creates dependency to a certain extent, and most importantly, is based on an oral culture. The learning environment in schools is formal, impersonal, individualistic, uses universal standards and achievement norms, and is based on a literate culture. Primary discontinuities are developed by students who come to this country and whose culture has already been developed in their country of origin (Ogbu, 1982). In this case, the curriculum content is alien; in other words, "the school is isolated from the cultural sys-tem it is intended to serve" (Ogbu, 1982, p. 305). In many cases these disconti-nuities are mediated and eliminated with time. Secondary discontinuities, on the other hand, are more pervasive and harder to remove. According to Ogbu (1982), secondary discontinuities are the result of relationships between two groups, one of which maintains a dominant status while the other is relegated to a caste-like state. For the most part, caste-like groups are those who were incorporated into U.S. society involuntarily, face job and status ceilings (a form of controlled social mobility), and whose socioeconomic problems are explained through discrimination. In the United States, the groups that hold this caste-like position, according to Ogbu (1982), are African Americans, Native Americans, Mexican Americans, and Puerto Ricans.

While Ogbu's cultural discontinuity theory attempts to explain the educa-tional experience of some children from so-called caste-like groups, it fails to explain why others who belong to these groups succeed in school. In the 1990s, Ogbu developed the notion of oppositional cultural frames of reference or oppositional culture. Oppositional culture refers to the idea that "under cer-tain historical conditions, forced assimilation and racism, do small cultural dif-ferences get 'inverted' into large cultural barriers that lead to school failure" (Foley, 1991, p. 67). Ogbu (1995) refers to oppositional culture as a way for caste-like groups to "outdo" those in mainstream culture who think negatively of them or put them down. According to Foley (1991), Ogbu's notion of oppositional culture looks upon ethnic expressions as negative and dysfunctional.

In his study with British students from working-class families, Willis (1977) concludes that students from working-class families reject the cultural capital of the school that values mental labor in favor of manual labor. His argument is that by doing so, students from low socioeconomic classes help to perpetuate their position in society. However, Willis's perspective fails to look at societal and institutional factors that might influence students' attitudes and, at the same time, reaffirms the idea that the poor are to be blamed for their situation for failing to live up to societal expectations.

In her work with Punjabi students, Gibson (1988) developed the notion of selective cultural assimilation, or what has become known as assimilation without accommodation. Selective cultural assimilation refers to selecting and assimilating to mainstream American culture, while simultaneously retaining a great deal of the native culture. Portes (1991) developed a similar concept he called segmented assimilation. Segmented assimilation can be applied to groups like the Punjabi students who assimilate to the maximum extent possible without losing their native culture.

Portes (1993) has also applied this concept to Haitian students in Miami. According to Portes, the generally accepted notion that immigrants who come to the United States should "melt" into American culture is no longer a valid argument because of the heterogeneity of adaptive behaviors. In the case of Haitian students, they find a dichotomy between parental expectations for success in their native culture and inner-city life. Ostracism of their language and culture leads Haitian students to adopt the inner-city African American values that, in many cases, carry as "a common message the devaluation of education as a vehicle for advancement . . . a message that directly contradicts the immigrant parents' expectations" (Portes, 1993, p. 249–250).

Other researchers have focused on the social and institutional aspects in school and the community that contribute to the maintenance of the status quo of certain groups. Mehan, Hertweck, and Meihls (1986) talk about the notion of a social construction of failure in relationship to children's school performance. According to Foley (1991, p. 74), the social construction of failure, defined as a "'mediating mechanism' in everyday institutional practices such as ability grouping, tracking, evaluation and counseling demonstrates how educational practitioners and students regularly 'construct' school failure." Mehan, Hubbard, and Villanueva (1994) have used the term reproduction theory to explain why children from working-class families grow up to hold working-class jobs themselves. According to Mehan and colleagues, "reproduction theory suggests that inequality is the consequence of capitalist structures and forces that constrain the mobility of lower class youths" (1994, p. 92).

The definitions of social and cultural capital suggest that each theoretical perspective focuses on different characteristics. Cultural capital refers to characteristics inherent in the family group (i.e., the language spoken, material resources, etc.) that can contribute to a child's education. Social capital, on the other hand, refers to resources outside the home to which the individuals have access (i.e., employment, social contacts, etc.).

CULTURAL CAPITAL AND SCHOOLING

In the 1970s, Bourdieu (1977) used the term cultural capital to refer to circumstances in which social power and privilege are obtained through particular mechanisms or socially accepted behaviors, in this case education. From a cultural capital perspective, schools are perceived as institutions with the primary function of maintaining a culture that perpetuates the position of certain groups in society. According to Bourdieu,

> the educational system reproduces all the more perfectly the structure of the distribution of cultural capital among classes . . . in that the culture which is transmitted is closer to the dominant culture and that the mode of inculcation to which it has recourse is less removed from the mode of inculcation practiced by the family. (1977, p. 493)

In other words, schools function from the premise that all children enter school "endowed with a system of predispositions" that allows them to learn successfully what is being taught (p. 494). Furthermore, this assumption presupposes that the cultural capital expected and taught by schools is that which is "adequate" or appropriate to survive in society. This perspective automatically denies the cultural backgrounds and strengths that students from diverse family backgrounds bring with them to the schooling process.

Lamont and Lareau (1988) define cultural capital as "institutionalized, i.e., widely shared, high status cultural signals (attitudes, preferences, formal knowledge, behaviors, goods and credentials) used for social and cultural exclusion" (p. 156). Lamont and Lareau distinguish between social and cultural exclusion by suggesting that social exclusion refers to exclusion from jobs and resources while cultural exclusion refers to exclusion from high status groups. Exclusion, Lamont and Lareau believe, is one of the key elements in Bourdieu's (1977) theory. In this sense, exclusion is seen as a type of power and control often used to dehumanize and alienate individuals and groups. "It is a power of legitimizing the claims that specific cultural norms and practices are superior, and of institutionalizing these claims to regulate behavior and access to resources" (Lamont & Lareau 1988, p. 159).

While cultural capital, as defined by Bourdieu and others, stresses the use of high status symbols for the inclusion or exclusion of individuals from high status groups, social capital has been used to refer to "social relationships from which an individual is potentially able to derive various types of institutional resources and support" (Stanton-Salazar & Dornbush, 1995, p. 116). Applied to education, role models and school counselors are the most common form of social capital for children. According to Lareau (1987), there is a generalized perception that there are social and cultural elements (capital) that some families have that facilitate compliance and communication with schools. Parents who speak standard English; are knowledgeable of what is taught in schools; have computers, encyclopedias, books, and access to the right resources; and are able to help their children with homework are most likely to comply with school requirements and to provide their children with the social capital (and cultural capital) that schools expect. Whereas families that do not possess these characteristics are not only pushed out of the system but are regarded as unable to take on the role that schools expect.

The argument developed thus far points to the fact that schools function to perpetuate the status quo of certain groups—those who comply with the expectations carry on and support the system. Those who do not comply with the expectations, become alienated and the target for social programs designed to fix what is wrong with them. Murgia (1995) suggests that "education . . . [rather] than being an equalizer of society, . . . exacerbates original inequalities" because individuals who enter schools with the right "social [and cultural] capital acquired at home do well in schools, [while] those with little of the required social capital are forced out" (p. 305). Poor and ethnically diverse families are seen by schools as not valuing education because they are perceived as not sharing the same values as those shared by members of the mainstream culture (Lareau, 1987).

It is important to stress that Murgia's (1995) argument is not that children from low socioeconomic or ethnically diverse families do not have social or cultural capital, but rather that the social and cultural capital they have is not valued in schools. Furthermore, Murgia (1995) adds that children fail in school not because it is an "inevitable reality" but because policy makers determine what is taught in schools, the language in which it is taught, and the content of the texts used for instruction. The argument then follows that policy making in this respect is exclusionary of certain groups and predisposed to favor others (Lareau, 1987; Murgia, 1995).

Stanton-Salazar and Dornbusch (1995) suggest that children from white, middle-class families have access to socially accepted role models and are better informed by school counselors. Poor and ethnically diverse children are disadvantaged in this aspect, because they are not raised with the same concepts as white, middle-class children, thus they are not taught by their parents to pursue certain socially accepted behaviors (Lareau, 1987; Stanton-Salazar & Dornbush, 1995). Furthermore, they are perceived as not having access to "socially accepted" role models or that the contribution that they make is inadequate, that is, socially unacceptable.

There is no doubt that ethnically and culturally diverse parents do make a contribution to the education of their children; whether society decides to look down on their contribution or judge it "inadequate" is a different issue. According to Lareau (1987), most parents value education and desire their children's success. However, based on their social and cultural experiences (capital), all construct the path to success differently.

More work has been done in Europe than in the United States using Bourdieu's notion of cultural capital. Most of the work that has been done in the United States has centered around the notion of "cultural deficit"; that is, the idea that families who do not belong to the majority group are out of luck because they lack culturally appropriate tools to succeed. This notion serves as a powerful statement of the way our society works, on how society has worked out its own mechanisms to preserve the status quo of certain groups.

TEACHING TO CHANGE THE WORLD

Theories of social and cultural capital as described above point to a type of systemic cruelty that operates at a societal level. Education, many educators and researchers have come to believe, is one of the central mechanisms which society uses to preserve the status quo of certain groups and delegate others to dishonored and caste-like positions. *Teaching to Change the World* is the title of a recent book by Oakes and Lipton (1999), in which the central premise is that teachers are in an excellent position to reverse this tendency and make schools the site of the production of *social justice*. Oakes and Lipton describe the assumptions of their book and stance in which teaching for *social justice* and *good* teaching are inseparable. They define a social justice perspective on education the following way:

(1) It considers the values and politics that pervade education, as well as the more technical issues of teaching and organizing schools; (2) it asks critical questions about how conventional thinking and practice came to be, and who in society benefits from them; and (3) it pays particular attention to inequalities associated with race, social class, language, gender, and other categories, and looks for alternatives to the social inequalities. (p. xviii)

Education for social justice goes beyond the categories of race and ethnicity discussed in this chapter to encompass all categories that have been marked out to designate oppressed groups. Under the wide umbrella of social justice education there is enormous momentum gathering from educators, researchers, and scholars who have staked out their position on the side of creating schools that work toward more equitable societies, rather than schools that reproduce the status quo. From a social justice position, any stance that attempts to be neutral in an unjust society actually works toward the reproduction of unjust social structures. A social justice position is not a passive position, but one that explicitly works toward change.

Schniedewind and Davidson (1998), authors of *Open Minds to Equality: A Sourcebook of Learning Activities to Affirm Diversity and Promote Equity,* have created a masterpiece in social justice education which begins with the following paragraph:

We have a dream. We envision classrooms and schools that are communities where students and teachers feel secure and cared about and where all forms of diversity are respected and appreciated. Here people don't feel afraid or threatened by those different from themselves, rather they feel stimulated by new discoveries about diversity that they regularly make. These are democratic classrooms and schools where all students are treated fairly and have equitable access to resources and opportunities. We envision a similar society and believe that as students and teachers we have the potential to contribute to the creation of that society. (p. 1)

Schneidewind and Davidson (1998) believe that classrooms provide the ideal places for students to be able to participate in socially just communities. Classroom *process* is as important as classroom content. They describe a four-step process to establish a classroom community that promotes social justice. Each of these steps is supported by a chapter in their book, which is full of excellent activities to promote and establish this process. These steps include:

Step A. Create an Inclusive, Trusting Community Where Students Appreciate Diversity in the Classroom.
Step B. Enable Students to Empathize with Others' Life Experiences and Explore Why and How Inequality Based on Difference Exists
Step C. Help Students Examine Discrimination in the Institutions in Their Lives and See How it Has Effected Them
Step D. Empower Students to Envision and Create Changes to Foster Greater Equality. (p. 2 & 3)

Schneidewind and Davidson's book is a rich resource which goes beyond learning about social justice to participating in working toward social justice in community. This process begins in reflection on one's own social identities and broadens out to include others. It involves students in understanding and recognizing social injustice and in working toward social and personal change. Participating in the kinds of activities in *Open Minds to Equality* (meant to supplement standard curricula) involves both students and teachers in a process of self and social transformation.

Educators who would choose to engage in social justice education are most often the ones who have become sensitive to issues of social injustice and are willing to do the difficult, though rewarding, work; to be involved in being change agents. Many teachers, however, who are steeped in more traditional notions of education and mainstream culture, have a difficult time *seeing* or *feeling* the social injustice in traditional forms of education.

COLORING THE SPACES IN TEACHER–STUDENT RELATIONSHIPS

In Chapter 1, Smith and Paul evoke the popular metaphor of "space" to talk about the relationships between teachers and students. This space, teachers all too often assume, is somehow transparent, and when we gaze across it at our students and they at us, we see each other clearly, simply as we all are. And yet, if we are to take into consideration the theories of cultural difference and social capital which have been described at length in this chapter, when teachers and students come from different cultural and social backgrounds, it is important that teachers understand that the spaces between themselves and their students often contain different shades of meaning, which are not, by any means, transparent.

> A prerequisite to accomplishing [a] multicultural vision of a utopian American society is to bring diverse ethnic and racial students together in public schools. . . . In order to have such an education, more than the physical presence of a racially and ethnically diverse student body is required. . . . it takes a considerable effort to understand views of the world embedded in cultures different from your own. Many times the beliefs of your native culture will consider such alien views to be products of ignorance, mistake, bias, or lack of understanding. In order to bring about appreciation of and respect for the culture of others, there must also be consistent and meaningful cultural exchanges that foster cross-cultural understanding, though not necessarily cross-cultural agreement. (Brown, 1995, p. 645)

Simply spending time in classrooms with children from diverse cultures and backgrounds does not automatically build an awareness of one's own cultural lenses. Teachers, in particular, can be somewhat insulated from learning from their students because of their traditional position of unquestioned power in the classroom and the assumptions that the teacher is the one who always knows best. Even teachers who enthusiastically embrace a multicultural or social justice curricula can be blind to their cultural lenses and unwittingly interpret cultural differences in their students as cultural or personal deficits.

Often teachers who resist addressing issues of diversity make statements like, "I see children, not ethnicity," or "I don't see color." While these comments are meant to describe a neutrality in relationship to all students and therefore *fairness*, it is at the same time a denial of students' cultural identities and differences, and of teachers' cultural lenses, biases, meanings, and values. This statement involves an assumption that one can be beyond the influences of culture and history, and therefore precludes the need to reflect on the meanings which color the spaces between students and teachers.

The following examples help make visible the kind of blindness to one's own cultural lenses which occur when teachers do not critically reflect on their own meaning making. Both of the teachers in these examples had very good intentions and both explicitly valued multicultural education. The first example involves a teacher in an ethnically diverse middle school. This teacher prided herself on choosing to live in a diverse neighborhood and teach in a school with a "majority of minority" students. She was a very dedicated teacher who lived in the same neighborhood as her students and welcomed them into her home.

One day, early in the school year this teacher overheard one African American student refer to another African American student as "nigger." Even though this was said affectionately in a private discussion between the two, the teacher cautioned the students that this kind of language would not be tolerated in the classroom, that it was "inappropriate." The students attempted to explain to her that this was the language used in their families and their neighborhoods and was not considered an insult when used among blacks. The teacher went into a long history of the negative meanings of the word and insisted their using it was both a sign of ignorance of African American history and disrespect of one another. The teacher threatened that further use of the term would result in the loss of some classroom privileges. One of the students became so angry that he cursed at her and was suspended from school. The teacher was truly perplexed at *his* ignorance as she blindly assumed she was in a better position to judge what was respectful and disrespectful in his culture.

The second example comes from a high school literature class in which there are 10 European American students and 2 African American students. The class is located in a special education school with a population that is 95 percent European American. The school principal has made a commitment to multicultural education and has invited guest speakers to do workshops on multicultural education for his teachers. In the literature class we are referring to, the teacher has selected excellent literature by African American writers. However, she has separated the two African American students from the rest of the class and only they read this literature. Recently, when the class got a student teacher, she was assigned to work with the two African American teens. They expressed anger toward the student teacher. They felt singled out and stigmatized both by their "separate" education and by being given the teacher who "wasn't really a teacher." However, the lead teacher silenced their pleas to be included with the rest of the group, telling them they needed to learn about their proud heritage. The underlying assumption was that *all* students would not have benefited from reading the literature by African American authors.

Both of these instances involved teachers who were well-intentioned, but who failed to do two important aspects in the *process* involved in multicultural education: critically reflecting on their own cultural lenses, histories, and beliefs; and listening, respectfully, openly, and attentively, to their students' stories. While trying to honor their students' histories and cultures, they did not honor their students' views.

Delpit (1995) describes what is necessary to transcend this sad state of affairs:

> To do so takes a very special kind of listening, listening that requires not only open eyes and ears, but hearts and minds. We do not really see through our eyes and hear through our ears, but through our beliefs. To put our beliefs on hold is to cease to exist as ourselves for a moment--that is not easy. It is painful as well, for it means turning yourself inside out, giving up your sense of who you are, and being willing to see yourself in the unflattering light of another's angry gaze. It is not easy, but it is the only way to learn what it might be like to be someone else and the only way to start the dialogue. (p. 47)

Teachers need to understand that good intentions do not automatically make us culturally sensitive. Without understanding what counts as care and cruelty to students and their families, it becomes impossible to know how to be a caring teacher. Often, what may seem like a caring stance from the teacher's perspective can feel like a disrespectful or discounting stance from a student's perspective. Social justice and multicultural education is not simply learning *about* diversity, it involves learning *from* and *with* diverse peoples.

Susan Benett (Mizell, Benett, Bowman, & Morin, 1993) sums up her first year teaching in an anti-racist school in a way that helps us understand the complexity of emotions and depth of learning involved for teachers in an anti-racist classroom:

> My first year introduced me to ideas I had never considered before, challenged beliefs which I did not realize were even there, stirred angers that had lain unexpressed. It was and remains a trying, tiring process. For me, it raised more questions than it answered, yet I am grateful that I have engaged in the questioning and the struggle. Philosophy has leapt out of the articles in magazines and actively into my life. I know that no matter what happens, whether I am hired back at Cambridge Friends School or go on somewhere else, I shall never be the same teacher again.

TEACHER TRAINING

To reduce the isolation of teachers from the cultural system of the student there is a need to create teacher-training programs that are responsive to the diverse school population being served. Teacher-training programs should stress first-hand cultural training/awareness. Approaching cultural understanding from a third-party "expert" is helpful in the sense that it can provide general information. However, teachers know that each one of the students in their classrooms comes with characteristics of particular households. One solution to the problem of blind stereotyping is for teachers themselves to become researchers of the children in their classrooms.

A project that has utilized this approach successfully is the Funds of Knowledge for Teaching Project in Tucson, Arizona. According to Gonzalez (1995, p. 3), "traditionally, teachers have visited students' homes either to discuss specific, often disciplinary, problems with parents, or to teach the parents how to better support their children's education." In the "funds of knowledge" project, teachers take on the role of the researcher and explore firsthand the family/community environment of the child. Funds of knowledge is defined as the "historically accumulated bodies of knowledge and skills essential for household functioning and well-being" (Gonzalez, 1995, p. 4).

According to Eisenhart (1995) caution must be exercised in the use of funds of knowledge when applied to usually stigmatized sectors of the society. Eisenhart pointed out that a study that explored homelessness only helped to reinforce the stereotypes students had about the poor and homeless. In other words, while the students learned more about homelessness, they did not "unlearn" their stereotypes. On a wider picture, Eisenhart points out that funds of knowledge is a useful approach; however, one needs to keep in mind the mainstream culture's definition of success and failure, and that for some students to be successful there needs to be some who are failures.

One type of support which teachers can offer students has been described by the metaphor of the scaffold. Lee (1992, p. 279) has carried out the idea further to the use of the "culturally sensitive scaffolding" or the "premise that the teacher uses the students' cultural knowledge as a foundation or support for school learning. The challenge is to identify what knowledge and practices in the family and community life have in common with what the school aims to teach."

Lee (1991, 1992) formulated three models of culturally sensitive scaffolding: (a) signifying and speakerly texts, which she has used with African American children, (b) talk story where she draws examples from the KEEP program in Hawaii, and (c) community funds of knowledge. According to Lee, these three models "support effective pedagogical principles that are consistent with the cultural and linguistic norms of ethnically diverse communities." She adds that the "models are based on pedagogical principles that are culturally specific yet applicable across populations of students" (Lee, 1992, p. 288). Lee's models exemplify Ogbu's notion of the dichotomy between the oral culture of the home and the print/written culture of the school, and the clash that emerges when students enter school. The clash, of course, is the result of the imposed value of the print culture over the oral culture. According to Lee (1992, p. 288), "the false dichotomy posed between print and the oral language serves a very detrimental role when the language of an ethnic community is belittled or castigated."

Other countries already stress the need for teachers to become an integral part of the community where the child belongs. Malka Shabtay, an educational anthropologist at Ben Gurion University in Israel, has formed a long-lasting relationship with the Ethiopian Jewish community and trains her students to become involved in the cultural and home environment of the families. Through this process, Professor Shabtay helps teachers become culturally sensitive to the needs and characteristics of children in this particular population (personal communication, 1995).

Teacher training can also benefit from focusing on ethnographic studies of diverse groups. Statzner (1994) recommends ethnographic research as a means of empowerment by allowing the voices of diverse groups to be heard. Some research has thus far focused on allowing minorities to voice their life experiences, either first-person or second-person accounts. More research needs to focus on diverse groups' perceptions of education as well as what the barriers or limitations are that prevent their participation in the educational process.

EDUCATIONAL PRACTICES: LANGUAGE AND COMMUNITY

In addition to immersing teachers in the communities of the students they teach, it is possible to involve the surrounding community in the classroom as well. Susan Britsch (1994) describes a project in which a preschool invited the elders of a small Native American community to work as partners to teach the children about the disappearing Tachi language. This project was piloted under the name of "Tachi as a Second Language" and was created out of the concern of parents in the Native American community that their children did not have enough opportunities to learn the stories and traditional values of their grandparents. In particular, they were concerned that the children did not have enough exposure to their ancestral language.

The goal of the program was not mastery, but to help the students become familiar and comfortable with the Tachi language. Two elder women worked with the children four times a week for about an hour a day. At first the teacher directed the activity, but as time went on the elders became more comfortable conducting the language sessions on their own. The teacher organized planning sessions with the elders which at first were more technical, but evolved into longer, informal sessions at which the elders told stories which helped recall their rich history. The teacher made it clear to the community that anyone who wanted to contribute to the students' learning could, and in this way an interweaving of community and school was established. This program gained the highest support and acknowledgment as can be seen in the following quote:

> At the end of the school year, the Tachi tribe's eldest male member (now in his nineties) paid a visit to the preschool to observe the children and to find out not what they were learning, but how they were learning. After conversing with the teacher, whose talk was interlaced with the Tachi she had learned from the elders, he concluded that the teaching was being done "the right way." He had not believed it, he said, until he saw it happen. This was the feeling of many community members, but as each person now encounters the children and their use of the language, Tachi becomes less removed from lived experience and more accessible to rediscovery within one's own life as a part of the lives of others. (Britsch, 1994, p. 204)

In this story of classroom and community we see a deep respect for the traditions, culture, and language of the students' community. This is in stark contrast to a recent court case in Texas in which a judge ordered a mother not to speak Spanish to her child at home because she was condemning her child to the life of a maid. While the judge reconsidered his position, the damage was done. However, we see similar sentiments expressed by opponents of bilingual education.

Bilingual education programs vary on a continuum from mainstream to maintenance. Mainstream programs are those that seek to help children learn enough English so that they can survive in a mainstream environment. Maintenance programs help children learn enough English to survive in a mainstream environment while at the same time emphasizing the child's native language and culture. Of the approaches, the maintenance model seems to be the most culturally sensitive but also the most controversial. According to Padilla (1991), some of the explanations proposed by the opponents of bilingualism in the schools and in the nation are not supported by what is actually happening in our nation. The English Only movement, according to Padilla (1991) is fueled more by a feeling of racism than by actual data.

The perception that immigrants do not want to learn English is not supported by people who understand that the only way to survive economically in this country is to learn English. According to McCollum & Walker (1992), while linguistically diverse students have a sophisticated communicative competence level in their own language, their label as LEP (Limited English Proficient) does not qualify them as ready to learn. Studies indicate that in most European countries children grow up learning at least two languages as a sign of educational achievement. The United States has often been criticized by the international community for the linguistic illiteracy of its students and yet the battle over bilingual education rages on.

Delpit's (1995) position on language diversity in relationship to black dialects adds another important dimension to thinking about the ways language is taught and valued in schools. Delpit denounces approaches that would suggest to students that their dialect is "wrong" or a sign of ignorance. However, she also cautions against a strict *process* approach which may honor students' rich dialects, but does not teach students Standard English forms. While well-intentioned, this practice limits students' access to the culture of power that requires standard English and may thereby limit students' economic possibilities.

Delpit (1995) provides some examples of how teachers can both affirm their students' own language forms and teach standard forms in non-threatening ways:

> Teachers need to support the language that students bring to school, provide them input from an additional code, and give them opportunity to use the new code in a non-threatening, real communicative context. Some teachers accomplish this goal by having groups of students create bidialectal dictionaries of their own language form and Standard English. Others have students become involved with standard forms through various kinds of role play. For example, memorizing parts of drama productions will allow students to "get the feel" of speaking Standard English while not under the threat of correction. Young students can create puppet shows or role-play cartoon characters. . . . Playing a role eliminates the possibility of implying that the *child's* language is inadequate, and suggests, instead, that different language forms are appropriate in different contexts. (p. 53)

Language and community are intimately linked. If teachers want to create caring communities in classrooms with students who are bilingual or bidialectal it is critical that the students' language is affirmed and celebrated in the classroom.

Teachers who set out to learn from students about their languages are in a much better position to teach standard forms in a mutual exchange. When teachers resist learning from students and families we must question the relationship between language and power. Students' identities and cultures cannot be divorced from their languages. When we invite students into our classrooms but ask them to leave their native language at the door, we take away the words that would allow them to speak not only their minds, but also their hearts.

CONCLUSION

One of the greatest questions that concerns teachers, researchers, and scholars today is, to what extent can schools be instrumental in bringing about societal changes through education? The focus of this text is on care and cruelty in the classroom. However, the questions brought up in multicultural and social justice education extends the questions of care and cruelty beyond the classroom and implicates schooling in the larger societal picture. Perry and Fraser (1993) describe an emerging vision:

> We would like to argue that school as a national institution, should prefigure the society we want rather than reinforce existing societal and political arrangements. And if the society we want is a democratic nation predicated on a diversity of racial and ethnic origins, we believe we have no choice but to revision our schools as multiracial, multiethnic, multigendered democracies. (p. 17)

Perry and Fraser go on to tell us that restructuring schools in ways that honor diversity would transform what it means to be a teacher. And indeed, they believe as we do, that teachers are central to the transformation of schools in the United States and in the transformation of American culture.

We began this chapter with a letter from a student who had been deeply hurt by a teacher's denigration of his social identity. However, there are many teachers who love the challenge of learning from their students about their rich cultures and languages. There are teachers who care deeply enough about their students to allow themselves to become learners about cultures, languages, and communities. There are teachers who take time to listen to their students and their students' families and who honor the stories that they hear and the languages in which they are told. There are teachers who inspire students to work hard to tackle the complexity of our multicultural society while honoring the rich cultural heritages they bring with them to class. The following letter attests to the important role teachers' love, understanding, and encouragement can play in the world of a child. What better place to start if we want to change the world?

Dear Mrs. B.,

You will always be a part of my memory of how scary it was to return to a different country and culture. I felt so afraid I knew more Spanish than English. I remember in reading, I tried so hard to say the words and they did not seem to come. It is still reflected in pronunciation of words today. I know I got really upset with you, but I learned an invaluable lesson. TO TRY. Boy has that stuck in my mind. I seem now ready to conquer the world. Thank you so much for your love, patience and understanding. Even though I was held back in second grade I still think it was beneficial to me.

Anonymous

REFERENCES

Bereiter, C., & Engelman, S. (1966). *Teaching disadvantaged children in the preschool.* Englewood Cliffs, NJ: Prentice-Hall.

Bourdieu, P. (1977). Cultural reproduction and social reproduction. In J. Karabel & A. H. Halsey (Eds.), *Power and ideology in education* (pp. 487–511). New York: Oxford University Press.

Bowles, S., & Gintis, H. (1976). *Schooling in capitalist America.* New York: Basic Books.

Britsch, S. J. (1994). The contribution of the preschool to a Native American community. In A. H. Dyson & C. Genishi (Eds.), *The need for story: Cultural diversity in classroom and community* (pp. 199–205). New York: Teachers College Press.

Brown, K. (1995). Revisiting the Supreme Court's opinion in Brown vs.Board of Education from a multiculturalist perspective. *Teachers College Record, 96*(4), 644–653.

Delgado-Gaitan, C. (1987a). Parent perceptions of school: Supportive environments for children. In H. Trueba (Ed.), *Success or failure? Learning and the language minority student* (pp. 131–155). Cambridge, MA: Newbury House.

Delgado-Gaitan, C. (1987b). Traditions and transitions in the learning process of Mexican children: An ethnographic view. In G. Spindler & L. Spindler (Eds.), *Interpretive ethnography of education: At home and abroad* (pp. 333–359). Hillsdale, NJ: Lawrence Erlbaum.

Delpit, L. (1995). *Other people's children: Cultural conflict in the classroom.* New York: The New Press.

Deutsch, M. et al. (1967). *The disadvantaged child.* New York: Basic Books.

Eisenhart, M. (1995). Promises and puzzles of culturally sensitive teaching. *Practicing Anthropology, 17*(3), 22–24.

Erickson, F. (1982). Taught cognitive caring in its immediate environments: A neglected topic in the anthropology of education. *Anthropology and Education Quarterly, 13*(2), 149–180.

Erickson, F. (1987). Transformation and school success: The politics and culture of educational achievement. *Anthropology and Education Quarterly, 18,* 335–356.

Foley, D. E. (1991). Reconsidering anthropological explanations of ethnic school failure. *Anthropology and Education Quarterly, 22*(1), 60–86.

Gay, G. (1993). Ethnic minorities and educational equality. In J. A. Banks & C. A.McGee Banks (Eds.), *Multicultural education: Issues and perspectives* (2nd ed., pp. 171–194). Needham Heights, MA: Allyn and Bacon.

Gibson, M. (1988). *Accommodation without assimiliation: Punjabi Sikh immigrants in an American high school and community.* Ithaca, NY: Cornell University Press.

Giroux, H. (1983). *Theory and Resistance in education: A pedagogy for the opposition.* South Hadley, MA: Bergin and Garvey.

Gonzalez, N. E. (1995). The funds of knowledge for teaching project. *Practicing Anthropology, 17*(3), 3–6.

Hess, R., & Shipman, V. (1965). Early experience and the socialization of cognitive modes in children. *Child Development, 36,* 869–886.

Kohl, H. (1994). *I won't learn from you and other thoughts on creative maladjustment.* New York: The New Press.

Lamont, M., & Lareau, A. (1988). Cultural capital: Allusions, gaps, and glissandos in recent theoretical developments. *Sociological Theory, 6,* 153–168.

Lareau, A. (1987). Social class differences in family–school relationships: The importance of cultural capital. *Sociology of Education, 60,* 73–85.

Lee, C. D. (1992). Literacy, cultural diversity and instruction. *Educationand Urban Society, 24*(2), 279–291.

Lesiak, C., & Jones, M. (Producers). (1991). *In the whiteman's image* [Film]. (Available from PBS Video, Alexandria, VA).

MacLeod, J. (1995) *Ain't no makin' it.* Boulder, CO: Westview Press.

Martinez, Y. G. (1994). *Narratives of survival: Life histories of Mexican-American youth from migrant and seasonal farmworker families who have graduated from the high school equivalency program.* Unpublished doctoral dissertation, University of South Florida.

McCollum, P. A., & Walker, C. (1992). Minorities in America 2000. *Education and Urban Society, 24*(2), 178–195.

McLaren, P. (1985). The ritual dimensions of resistance: Clowning and symbolic inversion. *Journal of Education, 167*(2), 84–97.

Mehan, H., Hertweck, A., & Meihls, L. J. (1986). *Handicapping the handicapped: Decision making in students' educational careers.*Stanford, CA: Stanford University Press.

Mehan, H., Hubbard, L., & Villanueva, I. (1994). Forming academic identities: Accommodation without assimilation among involuntary minorities. *Anthropology and Education Quarterly, 25*(2), 91–117.

Mizell, L., Benett, S., Bowman, B., & Morin, L. (1993). Different ways of seeing: Teaching in an anti-racist school. In T. Perry & J. W. Fraser (Eds.), *Freedom's plow: Teaching in the multicultural classroom* (pp. 27–46). New York: Routledge.

Murgia, E. (1995). Political capital and the social reproduction of inequality in a Mexican origin community in Arizona. In M. P. Smith & J. R. Feagin (Eds.), *The bubbling couldron: Race, ethnicity, and the urban crisis* (pp. 304–322). Minneapolis: University of Minnesota Press.

Oakes, J., & Lipton, M. (1999). *Teaching to change the world.* Boston, MA: McGraw-Hill.

Ogbu, J. U. (1982). Cultural discontinuities and schooling. *Anthropology and Education Quarterly, 13*(4), 290–307.

Ogbu, J. U. (1992). Understanding cultural diversity and learning. *Educational Researcher, 21*(8), 5–14.

Ogbu, J. (1995). Cultural problems in minority education: Their interpretations and consequences—Part one: Theoretical background. *The Urban Review, 27*(3), 189–205.

Padilla, A. M. (1991). English only vs. bilingual education: Ensuring a language-competent society. *Journal of Education, 173*(2), 38–51.

Perry, T., & Fraser, J.W. (1993) *Freedom's plow: Teaching in the multicultural classroom.* New York: Routledge.

Portes, A. (1993). Children of immigrants: Segmented assimilation and its determinants. In A. Portes (Ed.), *The Economic sociology of immigration: Essays on networks, ethnicity, and entrepreneurship* (pp. 248–279). New York: Russell Sage Foundation.

Rosenthal, R., & Jacobson, L. (1968). *Pygmalion in the classroom.* New York: Holt.

Schniedewind, N., & Davidson, E. (1998). *Open minds to equality: A sourcebook of learning activities to affirm diversity and promote equity* (2nd ed.). Boston, MA: Allyn and Bacon.

Sexton, P. (1961). *Education and income.* New York: Viking.

Stanton-Salazar, R. D., & Dornbush, S. M. (1995). Social capital and the reproduction of inequality: Information networks among Mexican-origin high school students. *Sociology of Education, 68,* 116–135.

Statzner, E. L. (1994). And Marvin raised his hand: Practices that encourage children's classroom participation. *Anthropology and Education, 25*(3), 285–297.

Stout, R. T. (1993). Enhancement of public education for excellence. *Education and Urban Society, 25*(3), 300–310.

Swisher, K., & Deyhle, D. (1989). The styles of learning are different, but the teaching is just the same: Suggestions for teachers of American Indian youth. *Journal of American Indian Education, 29,* 1–13.

Teachman, J. D. (1987). Family background, educational resources, and educational attainment. *American Sociological Review, 52,* 548–557.

Trueba, H. (1988a). Peer socialization among minority students: A high school dropout prevention program. In H. Trueba & C. Delgado-Gaitan (Eds.), *School and society: Learning content through culture* (pp. 201–207). New York: Praeger.

Trueba, H. (1988b). Culturally-based explanations of minority students' academic achievment. *Anthropology and Education Quarterly, 19*(3), 270–287.

Willis, P. (1977). *Learning to labor.* Farnborough, England: Saxon House.

6

ETHICAL QUANDRIES IN CONSTRUCTING TEACHER-STUDENT RELATIONSHIPS

Linda Houck
Florida Gulf Coast University

In the previous chapter, Martinez and Smith focus on how the relational space between teachers and students is impacted by racial, ethnic, and economic diversity. When students and teachers interpret the life-space of the classroom and the interactions that go on there in significantly different ways based on their own histories, the possibility for hurt feelings due to misunderstanding, unconscious racism, and fear increases. Even when we are sensitive and respectful toward differences in perspective, decisions about what to do in given situations can be difficult. This chapter focuses on the complex decision making process that is the heart of ethical deliberation.

Dear Mr. George,

It has been many years since I was a student in your second grade class. I was the quiet girl in the corner who was afraid to move for fear I'd come into your eyesight and be your next victim. Everyday I watched with horror as you picked the child who would be the brunt of your unhappiness, for a day, a week, a month. Every morning we all entered your class terrified. Who would it be today? Then there was that sign of relief we all felt—save for the one child who would be your target. . . . I remember one boy especially—his name was Timmy. I remember how kids lied to you and did mean things to make him cry. I watched you take their sides and ridicule, embarrass, and destroy this little boy. I was too afraid to say anything. I was only in the second grade and didn't want you to turn your focus on me. Why would you stay in a profession you so obviously hated? How could you look at yourself in the mirror everyday? You were supposed to teach us, you were supposed to be someone we could look up to. Instead you taught us fear, hatred and lack of compassion. What a legacy to leave behind.

A Former Student

Teachers are meant to be the "more knowledgeable other" (Combs, 1996) and caring, nurturing, fair, trustworthy, and ethical in their interaction with the children entrusted to their classrooms. Mr. George was the "more knowledgeable other" but his knowledge appeared to be in the areas of tyranny, power, anger, and revenge; hardly fitting the model we would like to think all teachers are molded from and aspire to be. How can teachers such as Mr. George remain in a helping profession? What went wrong?

One popular view of teaching is not a positive one. There are complaints in the media that teachers are overpaid for a short workday, and have extended vacations that include Christmas and the summer. Teachers are said to have an easy job with many perks; it's not for the brightest young people. It's not a coveted profession. As the old adage goes, "Those who can, do; those who can't, teach." In other words, anyone can teach, even the incompetent. This is not to imply that the teaching profession is uniformly dismissed, but this attitude is pervasive enough to raise its ugly head on occasion.

What is uniformly overlooked in this view, is the responsibility and power inherent to the teaching profession. Into the hands of the men and women in the ranks of "teacher," are placed vast numbers of our youth for a significant period of time both in terms of daily contact and contact over their childhood and adolescence. Viewed from the notions of responsibility and power, the teaching profession is both burdened and influential. The ramifications are far reaching and unfortunately can have devastating consequences. The power wielded by the teacher can be hurtful and the lessons learned can far outlast the reading, spelling, and math content presented. Teachers like Mr. George leave a legacy of failure to care, failure to nurture, and failure to demonstrate a love for learning. The influence teachers have over their pupils needs to be examined by practicing professionals and would-be hopefuls. The responsibility and power should fill these teachers with awe for their chosen work and a respect for the souls and minds of the children they lead. Indeed, education is not merely writing information on a clean slate, it is intertwined with daily decision making as to what is taught, how it is taught, and the relationship between this knowledge, the teacher, and the student (Noblit, 1993). In other words, ethical or moral decisions are many times at the root of the decisions made.

It seems clear that moral issues are intrinsic to and ubiquitous in teaching. The American political principle of separation of church and state does not mean that what goes on between teachers and students is morally neutral. What educators and parents fear most about bad teaching and celebrate most about good teaching are manifestations of fundamental moral virtues. Really bad teaching is "bad" in a moral sense; really good teaching is "good" in a moral sense. No amount of technical virtuosity in instruction can compensate for or excuse morally flawed, irresponsible behavior. (Clark, 1991, p. 263)

The description of Mr. George above evokes an image of that sort of "bad" teaching. From an ethical standpoint his behavior is "irresponsible."

The power that teachers appear to have is not absolute, however. Teachers are held accountable by many other authoritarian bodies--law, tradition, and moral codes. "To educate is to lead responsibly—influence students' knowledge, skills, and dispositions in ways that will serve them and their society well and to do so in morally defensible ways" (Clark, 1991, p. 251). The power of this relationship must be taken seriously. According to Bull (1993), from the student's perspective, the relationship with the teacher has several characteristics. It is compulsory: children must attend school. It is intimate: teachers have access to detailed knowledge about the child and his/her life. It is asymmetrical: this knowledge and responsibility are not reciprocated by the student. Finally, it is pervasive: the influence that a teacher wields is both over the child's present and future life. This unusual combination of characteristics makes the student particularly vulnerable to the teacher's actions, and for that reason, the teacher has an important moral responsibility toward the student. One wonders if the teacher in the letter above knew how vulnerable students were to his "methods" and if he even cared!

Since education is a mixture of academia and interpersonal relationships, it is "rife with ethical problems" (Howe & Miramontes, 1992, p. 1). Education is a constant balancing act among the individual student, parents, colleagues, policy makers, administrators, one's own personal integrity, and the profession of teaching. This is no easy task and requires an exploration of how one defines ethics and moral behavior, its relationship to pedagogy, and developing an "ethics of practice" (Sirotnik, 1991).

The purpose of this chapter is to examine these issues by looking at how ethical decisions are made in the classroom. The various moral theories are discussed and their relationship to practice explored. Examples of what one might call "unethical decision making" are examined through the teacher letters shared. Finally, the chapter discusses the place of ethical decision making in the professional development of both preservice and inservice teachers.

DEFINITION OF TERMS

It seems important then to define some of the terms that are used in this discussion. How are ethics and morals defined? Morals refer to right and wrong behavior, while ethics refers to the science of reflecting upon and studying morals (Turnbull & Turnbull, 1987). In other words, ethics is the study of morals. *Webster's Collegiate Dictionary* defines the terms similarly. Morals are "principles, standards, or habits with respect to right or wrong conduct." Ethics is defined in two ways that are applicable to this discussion. The first is similar to Turnbull and Turnbull (1987): "the branch of philosophy dealing with values relating to human conduct, with respect to the rightness or wrongness of actions and the goodness and badness of motives and ends." It is also defined as "moral principles." In much of the writing done in this area, the terms morals and ethics are often used interchangeably relying on the second *Webster* definition of ethics. This discussion also inserts one for the other since they are so closely related. An ethical decision and a moral decision are one and the same thing. Pedagogy refers to the technical work one does as a teacher; it is our methods, the "how"' of our instruction. Webster defines pedagogy as "the function or work of a teacher; teaching; the art or science of teaching; education; instructional method."

How are these three terms related? It's clear that morals and ethics deal with rightness and wrongness, goodness and badness of our actions and motives. In teaching, our methods or our pedagogy are our actions. Is our pedagogy right or wrong, good or bad? Is our pedagogy moral or ethical?

HISTORICAL PERSPECTIVE

Historically, the values that schooling is supposed to develop in students grew out of compulsory schooling and placing the mandate for deliverance of these values on public education. The purposes of schooling arose from different sources. There was pressure at the turn of the century to Americanize the immigrant, control child labor, and support for the belief that compulsory education was the progressive thing to do (Feinberg, 1991). Out of these pressures grew certain attitudes that shaped American education. The teacher became viewed as the expert; the school became the agent that socialized the child with the skills and attitudes required by a technological society; and the school was seen as fair—it allowed for equal access to status and reward. These themes have guided the structure and mission of public education. Most of the dilemmas in education revolve around these themes and the questions of who determines what is best for the child, who determines what is taught, and who determines what is fair. However, in our pluralistic society it would be very easy to become an ethical relativist in these regards, but many writers in this field believe that as a nation we can come to some agreement as to what our underlying principles or theories are that guide our work.

ETHICAL QUESTIONS

When considering our pedagogy from an ethical perspective, the underlying question is: Considering all perspectives, what ought to be done in a given situation (Howe & Miramontes, 1992)? Because so many factors play into the solution, the process is very complex, convoluted, and tentative. Also, ethical deliberations are not made only by experts and scholars; everyone faces ethical problems within daily living. Since we all face ethical problems, the solutions on the one hand can be viewed as subjective. Yet, if the input to the solution rests upon such things as "facts," law, personal beliefs, feelings, and personal and social conceptions of the good life, the solution itself is made up of various "lenses" or perspectives or voices. In other words, communities construct their understanding of ethical problem solving based on these voices. This collective voice arises from a sense of critical discourse. However, this may be only an ideal. To such writers as Bellah and his associates (1985), Americans may have become so entrenched in their "individual utilitarianism," that they may have let go of the ability to engage in ethical debate. That is, in order to truly find our moral principles, "public discourse" should be the forum that allows disagreement and discussion and gives voice to many perspectives in decision making. There are no easy ethical answers; the process is complex.

What we view as moral or ethical rises from our public discourse, our sense of what we are. Feinberg (1991) echoes the call for a "public philosophy" that Bellah and associates (1985, 1991) propose as necessary for a sense of identity and connection to the past.

> A public is created in the debate over its own constitution and over the struggle to give meaning to the events of the past and in the self-conscious awareness that a common self-definition is at stake in the debate. . . . the development of a public involves entrance into a critical dialogue in which respect for the interpretations of others is a part of the rational inquiry. (p. 178)

In the words of Bellah and associates (1985), "A free society needs constantly to consider and discuss its present reality in the light of its past traditions and where it wants to go" (p. 307). This discourse is the platform for society to ponder its past decisions and consider how to make present and future decisions. This is the place where an ethical point of view comes to be.

Ethics cannot be viewed as a set of rules or laws to be applied without any consideration of human relationships. Ethics is embedded in the application of these rules or beliefs or theories that communities have come to embrace as a result of dialogue. That dialogue is not merely a philosophical discussion of the pros and cons of this theory or that theory. The dialogue is a narrative, a story, where the community ponders the application of the theory to the complexity of human interaction, be that between a government agency and an auditor, a superintendent and a school board, a principal and a parent, or a teacher and a child. That's where ethics lies since ethics is by its nature communal or public given that ethics is humankind's way of negotiating relationships with others (Fasching, 1997). We develop our ethics based on who we are, that is, our life stories, our interaction with others, and to some extent the moral theories that have grown out of generations of life stories.

The next section of this chapter looks at the various moral theories and their recent evolution into an ethic of caring, where education is viewed as social in that relationships between people, not merely the passing of knowledge, are crucial. What is our connection with traditional moral theories and the now popular virtue-based theories? Morally responsible teaching carries all the burdens inherent in responsibility—difficulty, complexity, and sometimes painful and thankless work (Clark, 1991). How has our past molded our present ethical deliberations?

PRINCIPLE-BASED THEORIES

Broadly speaking, there are two kinds of ethical theories: principle-based and virtue-based. Both have exerted influence over our ethical decision making within the field of education. Principle-based ethical theories use basic ethical principles as the criterion for judging the rightness of actions (Howe, 1993; Howe & Miramontes, 1992). Their goal is to establish universals that can be applied across the board since they are viewed as objective and impartial. These theories are anchored in a mechanistic view of reality that the truth exists "out there," independent of the knower (Heshusius, 1989).

John Stuart Mill is a classic example of this type of thinking. He is known as a utilitarian. Utilitarians as a group believe that all ethics can be based on one principle: "Actions or policies are right when they maximize the total good" (Howe & Miramontes, 1992, p. 13). Another example of this perspective is Kohlberg's (1971) levels of moral development. His theory is based on moral absolutes through which people move regardless of their context. There is also a branch of this thinking called non-consequentialism that believes maximizing the good is subordinate to other principles, especially justice (Howe & Miramontes, 1992). Principle-based theories operate under the notion of the greatest good or the call for justice as the guiding principle.

VIRTUE-BASED THEORIES

Virtue-based theories "use a model of the virtuous deliberator" (Howe & Miramontes, 1992, p. 17). Virtue-based theories rely on relationships or what Aristotle calls "practical wisdom" (Bricker, 1993; Howe & Miramontes, 1992). Aristotle believed that members of a community would be able to recognize the person with practical wisdom intuitively just as they would be able to recognize a good physician or artist. This person would then be a model for comparison in making ethical choices.

There are two important features of the Aristotelian approach that have influenced current ethical theories. The virtuous deliberator is based on common values held by a community rather than abstract principles. Some theorists (Bellah, Madsen, Sullivan, Swidler, & Tipton, 1991; MacIntyre, 1981) maintain that the shared values of a community form the basis of ethical deliberations. The second feature is the emphasis on relationships.

Nel Noddings (1984) has written extensively on the role of relationship in ethical deliberations. She believes that the model for ethical decisions should be the caring person. She finds it incomprehensible to allow abstract moral principles to override the welfare of persons with whom one has established a caring relationship.

> An ethic of care starts with a study of relation. It is fundamentally concerned with how human beings meet and treat one another. It is not unconcerned with individual rights, the common good, or community traditions, but it de-emphasizes these concepts and recasts them in terms of relation. (Noddings, 1993, p. 45)

It is also important to realize that virtue-based theories are grounded in a much different view of reality. This view is characterized as a holistic view of the world built on relationships between the knower and the known. There is a reciprocal relationship between the two to the point where the known cannot be separated from the knower. Holism does not rely on universal truths but rather "tacit and personal knowing" (Heshusius, 1988, p. 64).

These different views of looking at ethical problems are both within our society. It could be argued that both have their place in our deliberations because they each serve their purpose. Broad general principles are necessary for a liberal society (Howe & Miramontes, 1992). For example, these principles prohibit discrimination and promote equal rights within our political process and educational system. Yet, there is still space for interpretation dependent on community and individual values. For instance, the Individuals with Disabilities Education Act (IDEA) mandates a "free and appropriate education" but the interpretation and application of that phrase is based on individual states and school districts.

LAW AND ETHICS

The legal system has become a vehicle for deciding issues that are ethical in nature. How can the law and ethics be related? These two concepts are clearly connected but they are not one and the same thing. In most cases, the legal thing to do is also the ethical thing to do. But in other cases, this may not be so if laws are defective from an ethical point of view. Since laws are by nature general and open-ended, particular cases may require ethical deliberations to fill in what is missing (Howe & Miramontes, 1992). Our special education system is based on case law (Overton, 1996). How IDEA is carried out is a reflection of the ethical deliberations grounded in civil rights and court cases. However, the following letter is a reminder that the law cannot be ever watchful, nor can it eradicate abuse. Mrs. O'Brien was a "legal" teacher; however, abiding by the letter of the law does not necessarily preclude ethical practice.

Dear Mrs. O'Brien,

I was a very shy girl growing up, and when I got into your 3rd grade class, I was beginning to open up and blossom a little. I know it's against the rule to talk, but on this one particular day I did. You then called me up to your desk, screamed in my face, and then grabbed my hair on both sides of my head, and jerked it back and forth. It was not only painful, but it was also very humiliating. How could you do that to a child, and know it was going to have an impact? This is, and will be, how I'll always remember you. Sad, isn't it?

You felt bad afterwards, and told me I could go out and get a drink of water. I didn't want it. It will never wash away your guilt. I hope my future students will remember me in a much more positive way than the way I remember you.

A Student

When looking at the practice of teaching, law is a poor guide since it can only set minimum enforceable standards. "Legal standards tell us what we are willing to coerce. What we should hope for should be different" (Strike, 1991, p. 202). The law does not specify ethical standards that are specific to the act of teaching. However, legal issues arch over any workplace. For instance, child abuse is not tolerated legally in any setting. In Mrs. O'Brien's case it may not have been tolerated in policy; but in reality it happened. She was legally credentialed as a teacher but her practice left a memory of abuse and humiliation.

The law does not deal with ethical issues inherent to teaching per se. Where does the law stand on indoctrination, grading and evaluation, and teacher autonomy? The law is unable to outline strict guidelines for enforcing an ethics for these issues because they are specific in nature. The laws that govern teaching intend to protect students from the most serious forms of abuse. Although this is important, it is insufficient as a guide to ethical teaching. Subtle abuse, losing control, and verbally attacking students can be just as damaging and serious;

however, as in the case of Mrs. O'Brien, it can exist behind closed doors and leave its damaging marks for years. What are missing are ethical standards that deal with the activities of teaching, respect for the values and intent inherent to the subject matter taught, and connecting the characteristics and actions of teachers with the moral purposes of education (Strike, 1991).

CODES OF ETHICS

Beyond the law, there exist codes in many professions that attempt to describe ethical behavior within that profession. Examples within the teaching profession include the National Education Association (NEA) code of ethics and the Council for Exceptional Students (CEC) code of ethics. Although they are worded very generally, they are at the same time much more specific than the laws discussed previously. Even though these codes are very broad, they are able to enhance ethical awareness and in that way encourage ethical decision making (Howe & Miramontes, 1992). In his discussion of codes, Sockett (1991) suggests developing a "code of practice," which would be locally developed between the community and the teachers so that it would be responsive to that community. The code would be referred to, displayed within the institution, and used as a guide for ethical decision making. It would grow out of the "public discourse" discussed previously and would relate to the community it guides. In effect, a code of practice would foster a partnership between public and professional control over the educational community. Sockett (1991) envisions a code of ethics emerging from these various codes of practice. The development of a code of professional ethics from codes of local practice would seem to avoid the pitfalls of codes discussed by Strike and Ternasky (1993). It is their belief that the development of codes of ethics removes the value of parental and student reflection from the process. Codes tend to make teaching more rule-bound and less caring. By empowering the community to develop codes of practice, the public discourse forces stakeholders to be reflective and an ethic of caring for the community as a whole could be nurtured.

ETHICS AND PEDAGOGY

Where does this discussion leave pedagogy? Is the answer found in principle-based theory, virtue-based theory, the law, codes of ethics, or codes of practice? It would seem that the answer lies within all of the above. Given the complexity of the decisions, the diversity of the students, and the values inherent in our methods and personnel, there is no "right" answer, but all of the perspectives discussed thus far help to expand one's ability to deliberate and reflect responsibly. In discussing this issue as it relates to special education, Howe and

Miramontes (1992) felt that special educators are tugged in two directions—principle and virtue—since they have a responsibility to both the individual child and the professional pull of consistency and impartiality. It would seem that with inclusion of special education students in general education to a greater extent, all educators will be pulled in both directions as they work with many more students who have special needs. For educators now and in the future, a grounding in ethical decision making may become even more critical; for them it truly may need to be an ethic of practice that develops out of their school community with an eye toward the traditions it values.

What then should be some of the elements of ethical pedagogy? The two authors reviewed, Sirotnick and Sockett, present what they felt was a synthesis of "basic principles of ethical practice." There are similarities between the two and they seem to blend both principles and virtues. In fact, these authors feel that both are necessary when developing an ethical approach to teaching. It is interesting that both authors felt that alone, the ethic of caring is insufficient. Both acknowledge the importance of relationship and care within the classroom community but both believe that it alone ignores important features of ethical decisions.

Kenneth Sirotnik (1991) develops his principles based on the synthesis of the positions put forth in *The Moral Dimensions of Teaching*. Teaching should foremost have a moral commitment to human inquiry. Thinking has become separated from action. The attitude of "That's interesting, but let's get on with it!" separates inquiry from doing. Does *America 2000* (Department of Education, 1991), and before that *A Nation At Risk* (National Commission on Excellence in Education, 1984) not point out a concern for a decline in thoughtfulness, reflective thinking, and the valuation of inquiry? Indeed, Rexford Brown (1991) calls for a literacy of thoughtfulness that he believes is rarely found even in progressive schools. Bellah and his associates (1991) say "it is clearly time to reintegrate cognition with a more fully human understanding" (p. 178).

Second, teaching requires a moral commitment to knowledge. This does not mean a body of facts but rather what a student constructs from the facts through explanation, interpretation, and understanding. In this way, knowledge is inextricably tied to inquiry. "A commitment to knowledge at a lesser level would be an affront to the human condition and would render pedagogy but a science of information retrieval" (Sirotnik, 1991, p. 300).

Third, an ethics of teaching must include a commitment to competence. This implies striving to do better what one has already tried to do. To Sirotnik this may be the definition of learning. It's an insatiable thirst to improve. "Moreover, it is a commitment that appears to be prudent; an incompetent society is not likely to be one that survives" (p. 301).

Fourth, ethical teaching is caring. In this sense, caring follows the lead of Noddings (1984, 1993) in that it refers to a deep relationship between people that is mutual, respectful, and trusting. Caring, though, must be qualified; it must be prudent and wise given the imperfections of humankind. Not all caring occurs at the individual level. The principle of justice allows for the broadening of the concept of care beyond individuals. Finally, ethical practice should have a commitment to freedom, well-being, and social justice.

These ideals are at the heart of our democracy and move ethics away from a relativist position. It implies a delicate balance between personal freedoms and societal jurisdictions (Thomas, 1991). If we were to evaluate the letters to teachers noted in this chapter, none would meet these criteria. How can we allow teachers without these ideals to interact daily with our children and then wonder why some of these children experience failure academically, socially, and behaviorally? America is a collection of multiple communities and we celebrate our diversity. Yet there is a community that transcends the many. As Bellah and associates (1985) articulated, it is a "moral ecology" held together by a political democracy and the values embedded within the system. This would demand that "any structures or practices that interfere with the simultaneous goals of equity and excellence, that perpetuate preexisting social and economic inequities, are subject to critique and elimination" (p. 310).

Hugh Sockett (1993) lists five virtues that he feels are at the core of professional expertise or ethical practice. He acknowledges up front that his approach is virtue-based but one could argue that these virtues also imply universal principles that can be applied to all pedagogy. Since teaching deals with knowledge, issues of honesty and deceit are paramount. Honesty in this sense refers to being true to the intent of the subject as discussed earlier. "This is morally important because deceit . . . puts a person arbitrarily in the power of another" (p. 65). For the teacher this means teaching the difference between fact and fiction and articulating a concern for the search for truth. This also means teaching an ethic of supporting one's beliefs; making a case for one's perspective among many. Establishing trusting relationships with students provides a foundation for demonstrating a deep-seated personal commitment to honesty.

Second, teaching and learning involve facing difficulty and taking risks; this requires courage. Trying to make teaching and learning easy ignores the fact that humans search for challenges to achieve. As noted in *Voices From the Inside* (The Institute for Education in Transition, 1992), learning should be both "joyous and rigorous." To do only one or the other is taking the easy way out.

Third, teaching demands care for the individual. For much of the school day, teachers have custody of the children entrusted to them. Care can be encouraged through dialogue and modeling. "Teaching people to care and to be full of care demands asking whether and in what ways the subject is worth caring for" (p. 81).

Fourth, fairness is necessary for democratic institutions and also one-to-one relationships. If children are to model fairness in their world they must experience it. How is time and attention distributed, how is discipline imposed, how does one relate to other faculty members? Finally, practical wisdom is a virtue that requires reflectiveness and judgment along with methods and content knowledge. This wisdom is context specific and changes with children and subject matter. Practical wisdom is connected to the other virtues, but in the sense that while one teaches, s/he questions whether the lesson is accurate, worth the risk, fair, and so on. It implies what Schon (1983) calls "knowing-in-action."

NEGATIVE PEDAGOGY

On further reflection, how can we as a profession explain or support some of the practices of teaching? Are they ethical from any perspective—principle, virtue, law, or code? The next letter deals with fairness.

Dear Mrs. Henson,

You were my 9th grade P.E. teacher. When I was in your class I was a small thin little boy, and you seemed to delight in singling kids like me out for harassment.

I will admit that I was not the most athletic kid, but you never even gave us a chance. When you assigned softball teams, you'd pick your favorite great athletes and divide them into two teams to play on the "real" field with you. Then you would send the other kids with some boxes for bases out into a field to fend for themselves. While you always played with the "better" kids, the retard squad (that's what we called ourselves) would be off in a field doing anything (you didn't care) as long as you weren't bothered.

I always hated you so much for singling me out at times as a non-example of how to play sports. However, you did teach me how not to treat kids who need a little more help than the others. You may be what sent me into the field I am in now—special ed: if so, then I thank you.

A Former Student

Is it moral to track students if one values social justice or fairness? What is the impact on a child of singling out the "non-examples" of how to play sports? The student above learned from being a "non-example"; however, the scars remain. For many students, do I.Q. tests and evaluation instruments support inquiry and knowledge? The use of rote learning does not seem to show courage or a moral commitment to inquiry. Does professional isolation support fairness to professional peers, caring, or a pursuit of competence? Can we continue to overlook the ego-bashing that existed in the classrooms of Mr. George, Mrs. O'Brien, or Mrs. Henson, or that caused a student to say, in *Voices From the Inside*, "This place hurts my spirit" (The Institute for Education in Transformation, 1992, p. 100)? Is the segregation of students and labeling of children always done with a sense of care and social justice? Finally, does the lowering of standards for some children show a commitment to competence, inquiry, and knowledge? Is our practice ethically defensible or blindly applied?

TEACHER EDUCATION

Why does practice sometimes seem to be unethical? Do not colleges of education across this country believe that they graduate people who have the ability to lead and motivate, not merely reward students based on a hidden agenda that only the teacher knows?

Dear Mrs. Johnson,

I know this isn't your name but you were my 4th year French teacher so I'll just give you that name.

You were a very boring teacher. However, I always tried to please my teachers and I did the same for you. I was a good girl, I smiled a lot and behaved in class. Unfortunately, I didn't learn anything because I wasn't motivated. You gave me an A in your class because I was a "good" girl. However, what about the kids who misbehaved? I think you gave them poor grades because of their behavior. That's not fair!

A Student

There may be many reasons for poor teaching and poor decision making. Our history is often a chronicle of man's inhumanity to man. Humanity has not always valued humanity; humankind is not perfect. More specifically, in light of pedagogy, methods are rarely taught from a moral perspective; they are considered devoid of morals.

Much of what we read in the literature of education and much of what we are told is "good" in the process of schooling is morally totally unexamined. Our conversation is dominated by mechanistic language: strategies, skills, time on task, and so forth. (Sockett, 1993, p. 14)

Teaching is a "moral craft" just as much as it is a "technical and procedural" body of knowledge (Clark, 1991). Until we examine our methods from a moral stance, they will remain technical and detached from our relationships within our school communities.

It could also be argued that as educators, we have not been asked to examine our moral principles. It may have been years since we have read or even seen the NEA or CEC codes of ethics. Without knowledge of, and experience in, ethical decision making, one may be frustrated with the whole process. This is not to be confused with being able to verbalize the elements of a virtuous man or the moral stance of Aristotle.

The connection between the interests of philosophers and the ethical behavior of educational professionals is sufficiently remote that it strains credulity to believe that people will behave better as a result of studying the products of academic philosophy about ethics. (Strike & Ternasky, 1993, p. 5)

In other words, courses in ethical theory will not make practice ethical. One must move from the abstract to understanding the theory embedded in a story rich with ethical dilemmas that mirror real life. The story or narrative makes the explanation of the ethical or moral principle clearer and allows the listener or reader to become the "disinterested observer" (Fasching, 1997). As the disinterested observer, the listener or reader doesn't see himself as the central character in the plot and is then able to see multiple possible solutions.

One approach to teacher education that seems to promote ethical decision making is the use of teaching cases within preservice and inservice teacher education (Shulman, 1992; Strike, 1991, 1993). Ethical decision making is then tied to practice and requires the student to reflect on the dilemmas and apply ethical principles within a community of learners. It allows for collaboration, multiple perspectives, and problem solving. It fosters personal reflection and accountability in the professional that goes beyond technical expertise. Reflection demands that one thinks about what one is doing, turns the thought back on the action and on knowing which is implicit in action (Schon, 1983). It connects thinking with knowledge and action which are goals of ethical practice. "The capacity to engage in . . . pedagogical judgment and action, therefore, rests as much on a combination of case knowledge and case-based reasoning as does .the capacity to reason ethically" (Shulman, 1992, p. 16). By engaging in reflection on teaching cases, educators can gain practice in exploring their beliefs, theories, and values within circumstances very similar to those they experience.

Human relationships are at the core of teaching and at the core of ethical practice. Morally responsible teaching requires that educators extend themselves beyond the letter of the law and technically effective teaching to connect with the child and use pedagogical practice that enhances what one has come to believe is ethical. One comes to those decisions by recognizing the relational nature of ethics. "Ethical awareness is generated by the experience of obligation to another human that is constituted by our coming to see our actions from their point of view" (Fasching, 1997, p. 117). An effort short of this is not "joyous and rigorous" nor responsible. This is a call to accept the importance of a "moral ecology" and the balance of relationships between society, pedagogy, schooling, and teacher education. "A mind is a terrible thing to waste"—let our practice ethically hear the call.

The letters highlighted here were all stories of hurt and unethical practice. Each letter writer carried with him or her an incident that may have happened many years ago but still seems to rub against the moral/ethical grain of the storyteller involved. Each letter writer came to take an ethical stance as a teacher very different from what they had experienced as a student. Their letter stories embodied glimpses of ethical awareness for both the letter writer and for us as readers. It is ironic that letters so full of hurt and lack of ethical care teach deep lessons about applying ethics to pedagogy. The writers learned firsthand about relationships from a non-example point of view. Each teacher learned the ethic of care from a very non-caring educator. This is the power of story and the power of relationships embedded in narrative. This is ethics.

REFERENCES

Bellah, R. N., Madsen, R., Sullivan, N. M., Swidler, A., & Tipton, S. M. (1985). *Habits of the heart.* New York: Harper & Row.

Bellah, R. N., Madsen, R., Sullivan, W. M., Swidler, A., & Tipton, S. M. (1991). *The good society.* New York: Alfred A. Knopf.

Bricker, D. C. (1993). Character and moral reasoning: An aristotelian perspective. In K. A. Strike & P. Lance Ternasky (Eds.), *Ethics for professionals in education* (pp. 13–26). New York: Teachers College Press.

Brown, R. G. (1991). *Schools of thought.* San Francisco: Jossey-Bass.

Bull, B. L. (1993). Ethics in the preservice curriculum. In K. A. Strike & P. L. Ternasky (Eds.), *Ethics for professionals in education* (pp. 69–83). New York: Teachers College Press.

Clark, C. M. (1991). The teacher and the taught: Moral transactions in the classroom. In J. I. Goodlad, R. Soder, & K. A. Sirotnik (Eds.), *The moral dimensions of teaching* (pp. 251–265). San Francisco: Jossey-Bass.

Combs, M. (1996). *Developing competent readers and writers in the primary grades.* Columbus, OH: Merrill.

Department of Education. (1991). *America 2000: An education strategy sourcebook.* Washington, DC: author.

Fasching, D. (1997). Beyond values: Story, character and public policy in American schools. In J. L. Paul (Ed.), *Ethics and decision making in local schools: Inclusion, policy and reform* (pp. 99–122). Baltimore: Paul H. Brookes.

Feinberg, W. (1991). The moral responsibility of public schools. In J. I. Goodlad, R. Soder, & K. A. Sirotnik (Eds.), *The moral dimensions of teaching* (pp. 155–187). San Francisco: Jossey-Bass.

Heshusius, L. (1988). The arts, science, and the study of exceptionality. *Exceptional Children, 55,* 60–65.

Heshusius, L. (1989). The newtonian mechanistic paradigm, special education, and contours of alternatives: An overview. *Journal of Learning Disabilities, 22,* 403–415.

Howe, K. R. (1993). The liberal democratic tradition and educational ethics. In K. A. Strike & P. L. Ternasky (Eds.), *Ethics for professionals in education* (pp. 26–42). New York: Teachers College Press.

Howe, K. R., & Miramontes, O. B. (1992). *The ethics of special education.* New York: Teachers College Press.

Kohlberg, L. A. (1971). From is to ought: How to commit the naturalistic fallacy and get away with it in the study of moral development. In T. Mischel (Ed.), *Cognitive development and epistemology* (pp. 163–175). New York: Academic Press.

MacIntyre, A. (1981). *After virtue.* Notre Dame, IN: Notre Dame University Press.

National Commission on Excellence in Education. (1984). *A nation at risk.* Cambridge, MA: USA Research.

Noblit, G. (1993). Power and caring. *American Educational Research Journal, 30,* 23–38.

Noddings, N. (1984). *Caring: A feminist approach to ethics and moral education.* Berkeley: University of California Press.

Noddings, N. (1993). Caring: A feminist perspective. In K. A. Strike & P. L. Ternasky (Eds.), *Ethics for professionals in education* (pp. 43–53). New York: Teachers College Press.

Overton, T. (1996). *Assessment in special education.* Upper Saddle River, NJ: Merrill.

Schon, D. A. (1983). *The reflective practitioner.* London: Temple Smith.

Shulman, L. (1992). Toward a pedagogy of cases. In J. H. Shulman (Ed.) *Case methods in teacher education* (pp.1–30). New York: Teachers College Press.

Sirotnik, K. A. (1991). Society, schooling, teaching, and preparing to teach. In J. Goodlad, R. Soder, & K. A. Sirotnik (Eds.), *The moral dimensions of teaching* (pp. 296–327). San Francisco: Jossey-Bass.

Sockett, H. (1991). Accountability, trust, and ethical codes of practice. In J. I. Goodlad, R. Soder, & K. A. Sirotnik (Eds.), *The moral dimensions of teaching* (pp. 224–250). San Francisco: Jossey-Bass.

Sockett, H. (1993). *The moral base for teacher professionalism.* New York: Teachers College Press.

Strike, K. A. (1991). The legal and moral responsibility of teachers. In J. I. Goodlad, R. Soder, & K. A. Sirotnik (Eds.), *The moral dimensions of teaching* (pp. 188–223). San Francisco: Jossey-Bass.

Strike, K. A. (1993). Teaching ethical reasoning using cases. In K. A. Strike & P. L. Ternasky (Eds.), *Ethics for professionals in education* (pp.102–116). New York: Teachers College Press.

Strike, K. A. & Ternasky, P. L. (Eds). (1993). *Ethics for professionals in education.* New York: Teachers College Press.

The Institute for Education in Transformation. (1992). *Voices from the inside.* Claremont, CA: The Claremont Graduate School.

Thomas, B. R. (1991). The school as a moral learning community. In J. I. Goodlad, R. Soder, & K. A. Sirotnik (Eds.), *The moral dimensions of teaching* (pp. 266–295). San Francisco: Jossey-Bass.

Turnbull, A. P., & Turnbull, H. R. (1997). *Families, professionals, and exceptionality.* Columbus, OH: Merrill.

7

THE MORALS OF
TEACHERS' STORIES

Terry Jo Smith
National-Louis University

Susan Perez
Cedar Crest Honors Academy

In this book thus far, we have addressed the space between teacher and student from students' memories of former teachers, and through theory and philosophy. Theoretical and philosophical approaches, while powerful and important means of organizing our thoughts and ideas at more abstract and general levels, do not often provoke strong emotion, as they usually occupy a space removed from context and people.

In the letters written to teachers, the vulnerability of reentering, through memory, the more personal spaces of student–teacher relationships is somewhat eased by the distance of space and time. In addition, because the writers of the teacher letters were students in the experiences they wrote about, they held less responsibility for the nature of the relationships they described. Although their status of student afforded them less power and more vulnerability while in the classroom, in examining their relationships with teachers through memories, they are at a decided advantage. If harm was done, it was not their fault.

In this chapter and the next we move into more perilous waters. We address the lived spaces of classrooms through teachers' stories and from teachers' positions. While teachers have more power in the classroom than students, they are situated within hierarchies where they are also in a position of less power than administrators, and often parents. Their stories reflect the complex positions they occupy.

In the previous chapter, Houck discusses ethical considerations and pedagogy from the position of moral philosophy. In this chapter we focus on the relationship between story and moral dimensions of education by examining the autobiographical writing of a few teachers whose stories of classroom life have gone beyond the usual audience of family and friends to become part of our greater cultural meanings through public-ation. We look at how teachers' stories help make moral aspects of education visible, and how the very act of telling their stories allows teachers to begin to take greater moral responsibility for their practices.

SPACES CREATED IN TEACHERS' STORIES

When teachers spin experiences into stories about schooling, they create texts that can provide insights into dimensions of education which have often been overlooked. Stories have *morals*, beliefs concerning what is good and what is not. Through story we can address moral dimensions of education from within the contexts of particular lives; lives that have feelings, lives that have histories, lives that exist within culture and community, lives that have gender, and lives that are connected to other lives through relationships which are often multiple, complex, paradoxical, and fascinating.

As we explore the images and meanings evoked by teachers in their stories, we focus on the values, politics, and beliefs infused in their construction. In addition, we explore their depiction of the social contexts of schooling; the institution, the system, and the spoken and unspoken rules that attempt to organize and define school culture. Teachers' stories offer bridges into classroom culture, into teachers' beliefs and theories, into the heart and soul of educational experience. As teachers story their experiences, they move into a place of author-ity (Gitlin & Russell, 1994; Tappan & Brown, 1991). This is a political move, for in telling one story, we often dislodge, counter, or at least question the "official" story. And this is a moral move, for in telling our stories we nearly always align ourselves with the "good" (Taylor, 1989).

Teachers' stories often have an explicit agenda. They address moral and political dimensions of education, dimensions we have often overlooked in our obsession to be scientific in our inquiry. Education is not experienced through scientific method, it is experienced through the lives of individuals and in relationships that occur within the contexts of community, culture, and institution. Story can take us there.

THE MERITS OF STORY

In recent years, several educational researchers, theorists, and philosophers have begun to embrace story as an important medium for inquiring into education (Ayers, 1992; Cochran-Smith & Lytle, 1993; Gitlin & Russell, 1994; Gitlin et al., 1992; Griffith, 1995; Isenberg, 1994; Noddings, 1991), as well as an important means of transforming education (Kincheloe, 1991; McLaren, 1989). Storying experience can help us understand ourselves and others (Cooper, 1991), can help us take responsibility for our moral actions (Tappan & Brown, 1991), and can help us break out of long engrained notions of "the way it is" (Lather, 1994). Beyond this, story can bring us comfort (Isenberg, 1994) and insight (Cooper, 1991), and provoke us to take action (Gitlin & Russell, 1994; Isenberg, 1994). It is through story that we breathe meaning into experience.

When students and teachers begin to tell their stories of schooling, we begin to participate in constructing what education means. Although this process is constrained by hierarchical structures and positivist philosophies of knowledge, story can take us beyond those constraints into new places of possibility. Story has much that recommends it, especially in light of a growing awareness of an urgent need to restructure education. For if we really want to re-imagine education, we need to explain, to situate the differences we imagine into stories in which they represent the "good."

Storying Difference

Bruner (1990) tells us that narrative is born in difference. When what happens is not what we expect to happen based on our folk psychology, we bridge the space between expectation and experience with a story about the difference that gives meaning to the unexpected. Bruner explains that when things go as expected there is no need to say anything; the meaning has already been determined; things are as they *should* be. When things do not meet expectations, narrative is used to explain the *difference.*

It is through cultural systems of interpretation that our lives make sense to us and to others. Our sense of ourselves, our everchanging autobiography, achieves meaning through participation in symbolic systems of culture. Narrative allows us to make connections between the ordinary or expected and the exceptional. Bruner (1990) tells us: "The function of the story is to find an intentional state that mitigates or at least makes comprehensible a deviation from a canonical cultural pattern" (p. 49). In this important function, narrative "mediates between the canonical world of culture and the more idiosyncratic world of beliefs, desires, and hopes" (p. 53).

In this view, by constructing new stories, we can construct new possibilities for education. Teacher's stories can function to facilitate educational change. Storying experience allows one the space to veer from the expectations ingrained in notions of "the way it is," to imagine the "way it could be." Story frees one up to act differently, to try new ways, because story can situate difference in contexts of thought, human intention, feeling, culture, and individuality, in which they have meaning and purpose. By telling their stories teachers allow us insight into their intentions, what they are trying to do in relationship to others. Bruner (1990) tells us:

> Insofar as we account for our own actions and for the human events that occur around us principally in terms of narrative, story, drama, it is conceivable that our sensitivity to narrative provides the major link between our own sense of self and our sense of others in the social world around us. The common coin may be provided by the forms of narrative that the culture offers us. (p. 69)

In educational discourse, the kind of language that has been considered legitimate in our *professional* culture has been largely an authoritative spectator language that aligns itself with The Truth and uses knowledge as control (Stone, 1992). In education, for the most part, theoretical language has been privileged and the language of story has been ignored (Griffith, 1995; Isenberg, 1994). Anita Plath Helle (1991) describes the dangers involved:

> Theoretical discourse has typically been language held by those in power, and it has often structured our reality by pointing to fixed and impartial frames of reference—hallmarks of the exclusive reliance on separate knowing. Once such references become a part of the a cultural code, they operate unconsciously to constrain rather than to liberate the construction of alternative standpoints. (Eagleton, 1983, p. 64)

When teachers tell their stories they move into an imaginative space in which they author their experience and in so doing begin to break free of the often unconscious cultural codes that constrain meaning. In their stories, they create themselves and their students, classrooms, schools, and communities based on their experiences, beliefs, and theories. Storying their experiences, teachers move away from relying on knowledge constructed separate from their classroom contexts into a place of connected knowing, and ultimately into a place of greater responsibility and freedom.

Storied Selves

Teachers' stories involve constructing versions of one's teaching self within the context of relationship and institution. These constructions of self help us know ourselves, reflect on our place, and provide us an opportunity to change ourselves. William Ayers (1992), describes several important dimensions that teachers' stories tell:

> Our stories are never neutral or value-free. Because they are always embedded in space and time and people, they are necessarily infused with values, forever

political, ideological, and social. Our stories occur in cultrual contexts, and we not only tell our stories, but in a powerful way our stories tell us. Interrogating our stories, then—questioning and probing our collective and personal myths—is an important pathway into exploring the meaning of teaching. (p. 35)

Carol Witherell (1991) warns us that when we don't continuously interrogate concepts of self, then worn out, reductionistic, reified concepts of self come to be considered "common sense"—an awfully powerful and pervasive kind of "knowing." In schools this has been translated into an uncritical reliance on psychometrics in lieu of dialogue and relational knowing.

Educational discourse, traditionally couched in spectator language (Stone, 1992), has often functioned to conceal self while providing authoritarian constructions of others via psychological and educational language. An emerging awareness that such practices are culturally oppressive and no longer morally defensible have come from many fronts: gay and lesbian theorists (Leck, 1994; Tierney, 1994), cultural theorists (Foster, 1994), feminist theorists (Fine, 1994; Lather, 1994; Morris, 1995; Stanley, 1990), and critical theorists, (Gitlin & Russell, 1994; Kincheloe, 1991; McLaren, 1989).

In their teaching stories, teachers construct versions of themselves and their students, and are empowered in the process. Weber and Mitchell (1995) describe this move as breaking away from powerful cultural metaphors. They tell us, "Teachers are not merely victims of society's cultural imagery. Although they are born into powerful socializing metaphors, some of them manage to break and recreate images while making sense of their roles and forging their self identities" (p. 26). In "Telling Our Stories: The Reading and Writing of Journals and Diaries," Joannne Cooper (1991) writes about how writing our life helps us to know it, create it, and change it. She sees teachers' stories, written in diaries and journals as holding the potential to transform education as teachers begin to "own" their stories.

> As chroniclers of our own stories, we write to create ourselves, to give voice to our experiences, to learn who we are and who we have been. Our diaries become the stories of our journeys through life, stories that are both instructive and transforming, in the telling and the listening. These stories, these myriad voices, then serve to instruct and transform society, to add to the collective voice we call culture. Diarists, then, both as researchers and research subjects, begin to heal themselves and the split society has created between subject and object. Thus, diaries, these small, insignificant objects filled with the simple words of our lives, can serve to make us whole. (p. 111)

MORAL STORIES

Stories almost always have morals. The author takes positions within the narrative as to what comprises the "good." Often stories contain moral dilemmas in which the actors must make choices and take action. Narrative is a way of making sense out of experiences by placing events wtihin contexts which give them meaning, describe the intentional states of the actors (Bruner, 1990), define relationships between self and others (Cooper, 1991; Helle, 1991), identify moral dilemmas and describe moral positions and practices (Tappan & Brown, 1991). Tappan and Brown (1991) explore the relationship between narrative and moral development.

> Rather, we want to return to the issue of narrative and argue, based on three related assumptions, that when we make moral choices and decisions in our lives, we represent those choices and decisions, and give them meaning, primarily by telling stories about them. Narrative thus becomes a very important means for understanding both moral experience and moral development. (p. 177)

Tappan and Brown suggest that in constructing narratives about our experiences, we promote our moral development because in the act of authoring we become aware of, and take responsibility for, our own moral stories. In the process of imbuing narrative with moral value, we assert our moral authority. We moralize in our stories, and often align ourselves with the good (Taylor, 1989) as we recognize, interrogate, and claim authority for our moral perspectives. This "owning" of moral stories in education counters the unspoken ethic of "morality as conformity" which is a hallmark of hierarchical institutions (Spence, 1980). It is through recognizing our own moral authority in our storying of experience that we can counter the temptation to abdicate moral responsibility to those in authority. Through writing our moral stories we forge our moral identities and leave ourselves less vulnerable to participating in cruel acts.

STORIES OF PROTEST

Jane Isenberg (1994) has studied teacher autobiography extensively and concludes that teacher narrative should be considered both research and literature. In her studies of teacher narrative, Isenberg began to get a sense that she had seen a similar genre before. It dawned on her that teacher narrative held many commonalities with slave narrative. She clarifies that she is not suggesting that the severity of the suffering and oppression is the same with teachers and slaves, only that their political configurations and avenues of liberation have similarities worth noting in an attempt to understand dimensions of teaching which are political, though often covertly so.

Isenberg compares teacher narrative and slave narrative on several counts. She begins by pointing out that most teacher narratives are told by "angry authors who describe the suffering of a disempowered constituency in the hope of ending that suffering. They are constructed around crises of literacy, identity, and control and operate within constraints and conventions that are politically determined" (1994,

p. 105). Isenberg points out that slave narratives are autobiographical and yet what is central to them is slavery rather than self. This is true of teacher narrative as well. They are autobiographies about teaching and schools and the lives that come together in those places, concerned with an institution from the position of self, rather then self primarily. Both are a kind of protest literature, written within a heavily stratified context in which class bias is prevalent. Isenberg (1994) makes a comparison on many points:

> Like slave-narrators, teacher-narrators are usually politically motivated; teacher-authors use their own experience to bear witness to terrible, ludicrous, or simply counterproductive things that happen within schools. . . . Like the exslave-authors, teacher-writers are representing an inarticulate constituency, children and teenagers, who suffer as a result of the failures of our educational system and the people who prescribe and implement its policies in a society which routinely devalues children. . . . Also, like exslave-authors, teachers themselves are former students, marked for better or worse by their years on the other side of the desk. (p. 110)

Isenberg depicts teacher-narrative as a type of testimonial to the hostility that permeates school environments with teacher-writers attempting to bring to social consciousness their own struggles and the struggles of their students as evidence of oppressive practices which often have been concealed and repressed both in educational practice and research. One area where teacher-narrative and slave-narrative differ is in the social realities they attest to. Slavery has been abolished, but the oppressive conditions within schools have not been dramatically altered.

Isenberg (1994) believes that teacher-narratives can play a critical role in politicizing new teachers. She writes:

> Therefore, it is now more crucial than ever to actively engage aspiring and developing teachers in productive thinking about the nature of their teaching, and that of schools. This intellectual and emotional involvement can be fostered through the use of teaching narratives, which are, in fact, designed to involve their readers and move them to action. Clearly, these provocative autobiographical narratives are a precious legacy from which we still have much to learn. (p. 130)

FRAMING TEACHER'S STORIES

In the previous sections we focused on theories and beliefs about story. One purpose for this was to construct a few possible theoretical frames for looking at teachers' stories. This framing can serve as a way to focus our thinking and seeing. For example, based on Bruner's (1990) ideas, we might ask how our writers use story to make sense of things which go outside of the bounds of expectation, that is, how do these teachers story *difference?* We might as easily frame our teachers' stories by highlighting dimensions of story that Ayers (1992) describes, by focusing on what the story tells us of the writer's values, beliefs, and politics. Based on Tappan and Brown's (1991) work, we might look for the moral dilemmas identified by the writers, that is, what they identify as good and bad, as well as what moral action they took based on which beliefs. Based on Isenberg's (1994) work, we might look at teacher's stories and ask "what are these teachers protesting?" Or, in relationship to Spence's (1978, 1980) ideas we might ask "what are the structural barriers to liberation?"

In the following sections we look at excerpts from teacher autobiographies. Our purposes in doing this are many. First, the stories are rich in moral themes, which are only beginning to be addressed in our professional studies but are of great importance if we are going to restructure and re-imagine education in more equitable ways. Secondly, we would like to show, using the frames briefly sketched above, some ways to read teacher narratives that take us beyond just enjoying a good story, to being moved to action. That is, we want to explore what can be learned from these stories that will help us be more aware and caring educators who can work together to create an educational system that is more responsive to individual needs and less driven by institutional needs.

One thing that is frequently particularly significant to those who author their experiences in schools into stories about student–teacher relationships, is that these relationships are extremely powerful and important in our lives. These stories tell of personal, human dimensions of learning which shape our beliefs about ourselves and others, about schools, about society, about race, culture, power, and morality. These lessons are the heart's lessons, and they inevitably stay with us long after our vaguest remembrance of the Pythagorean theorem has gone. It is to this space we turn, a vulnerable and often hidden space of relationship. When we story it, we create it, and ultimately take responsibility for it.

A STORY OF MORAL RESPONSIBILITY

In *Girls at the Back of the Class,* LouAnne Johnson (1995) writes a soul-searching account of her classroom experiences in a southern California school district which is rife with racial and social tensions. Her courage and raw honesty take us into personal spaces, spaces of pain, joy, and genuine learning, though the lessons learned are often about harsh realities. From beginning to end, her story is compelling. Her moral conflicts are complex and as it is in life, often without satisfying solution. In her stories she takes us on a journey into the intense sadness, but also the intense joy, many teachers face when they work with children whose lives are often battered from poverty and social oppression. Her moral conflicts often arise out of her unwillingness to participate in the institutional abuse of the students she grows to love.

It is difficult to pick a single story out of the many pages of rich narrative she tells. We settled on a story about sexism, from which she took the title of the book.

We chose this story because it is an excellent example of self-learning involved in becoming a caring teacher. It is also an example of how theory and practice can be bridged in the life and writing of a teacher. Plus, it breaks an important myth about sexism: it does not only occur between genders, but within genders. This was not a male teacher who overlooked "the girls in the back of the class" as they silently slipped away, but a caring woman of the 1990s who had been blind to her own sexist attitudes. This is a story of her dawning social awareness and of taking moral responsibility for how she sees and treats others.

This story begins at the end of another one, just like life. Johnson was telling about a boy named Cornelius who came into her class furious one day. He ranted and raved about being harassed by the police because he was a young black male. Reflecting on this incident and similar incidents, Johnson began to wonder about the *girls* in her class:

> Looking back, I wonder whether Simoa Mariposa tried to get my attention, too, whether Cornelius and Rico outshouted her, or whether she simply slipped out of sight so quietly that I didn't even notice she was slipping until it was too late. And I wonder whether that's what happened to the other girls in the back of the class, the original Academy girls who had disappeared somewhere between their sophomore year and graduation. I wonder whether they believed they were less important than the boys, whether they simply accepted the pain in their lives with less protest. Or did I pay less attention to their protests? (Johnson, 1995, p. 122)

In her reflection, Johnson has identified a moral dilemma in which she does not align herself with "the good." She courageously forges on, sculpting with words her own theories of the *differences* between male and female students. She writes:

> I would like to believe that I would have heard Simoa ask for help, even if she whispered. But now I wonder whether that is what she did, whisper; whether that's what girls do, whisper while boys shout; whether the girls whisper because they don't really want to be saved from themselves. (p. 123)

Johnson looks further into her experience and through her connected knowledge refines her theory about the differences between the girls and boys she works with.

> Boys drop out because they want to work, or because they can't tolerate taking orders anymore, or because they refuse to develop the self-control necessary to restrain themselves from smacking anybody who makes them mad, or because they are in a hurry to start their careers as criminals. When they drop out, boys usually end up on the street or in jail, and they know this, and they make a lot of noise on their way out in the hopes that we will stop them.
>
> Girls on the other hand, usually leave school in search of True Love, or because they believe they have found it. They are seduced by sex into thinking that the happy

ending is within reach, if only they didn't have to waste their time being educated. So they get pregnant and quit school, or quit school and get pregnant, or become so pregnant with their delusions that they quit school. Girls leave more quickly and quietly than boys do. Girls wring their hands in quiet desperation for a few weeks, then disappear. (pp. 123–124)

One of the beauties of teachers' stories is that the theorizing is particular to specific contexts. These differences between boys and girls are not presented as universal truths, but the theorizing of a teacher, based on her connections with her students. Even as such, they do not represent the *final truth* in the matter, as we shall see as Johnson further interrogates her stories.

Maybe this is just my perception, my rationalization for why so many girls silently slipped away from me. I don't know. But I do know that I will never quite forgive myself for forgetting to talk to Simoa after class that day when she said she worried about her father "stomping" on her. I still have the slip of paper, the one on which I jotted her name to remind myself to talk to her immediately, but I forgot about it until that night as I changed out of my clothes and emptied my pockets. (p. 124)

Johnson, upon further soul searching, does not believe her theories of *difference* between boys and girls can account for her own *different* treatment. She accepts responsibility for her own moral actions and continues her journey to try to understand and change her own behavior. In her journey for self understanding and moral enlightenment she looks to research journals for guidance.

As a pot of pasta was busy noodling water all over the top of my stove, I sat in the living room and read an article in an educational journal that cited several studies indicating that most teachers favor boys over girls in the classroom. Teachers spend more time with boys, the author claimed, and pay more attention to them during lessons. (p. 124)

Johnson takes this research and weaves it in with her connected theories.

That's entirely possible, I thought, and probably because girls usually get the message more quickly. A frown, a cough, a whisper is usually enough to convince the girls in the class to put away their makeup, stop passing notes, or save the giggles for later. But boys very often view eyebrow raising and throat clearing as encouragement to continue their misbehavior, not as a deterrent. (pp. 124–125)

After grounding the facts and figures she read about in the research journal in her own theory and experience, Johnson circles back to the article once again.

Teachers smile more at boys, the journal article said, and they call on boys more often to answer questions during class. And they tell girls to be quiet, even though, statistically speaking, girls spend less class time talking. The saddest thing, the article concluded, was that the teachers who favored boys most were the very teachers who took pride in their equal treatment of both genders. (p. 125)

Here comes, full force, the painful realization.

That would be me, I thought. Was I one of those deluded teachers? Did I spend more time and energy on my male students? Was that why I hadn't noticed until graduation day that only five girls from the original academy class left Parkmont High with their diplomas? . . . Of the five girls in the same graduating class, two were black, none was Hispanic. Nobody had ever mentioned those sad statistics. Sadder still, I don't think anybody, including me, had even kept count. Why hadn't I? (p. 125)

Surprised at her own blindness, Johnson delves deeper to try to understand why. This time she circles to her personal history, remembering her experiences of being at the other end of derogatory sexist treatment.

After serving nine years in the macho, male United States military, where I witnessed and experienced daily doses of gender bias, from subtle slights intended to undermine my self-confidence to blatant abuse designed to make me give up and go home, why wasn't I more aware of gender bias at my own school, even in my own classroom? (p. 126)

Once she locates her feelings associated with sexism, she searches for underlying beliefs that had supported her behavior. Johnson cleverly shows us what "it all boils down to."

All the water boiled away and my fettuccine glued itself permanently to the bottom of the pot as I pondered the possibility that I had somehow been brainwashed into believing that it was my job as a teacher of at-risk students to save minority males at all cost, to save white males whenever possible, and to let the females—regardless of race—fend for themselves. (p. 126)

In writing her stories, Johnson developed a keen moral consciousness. She does not write herself as the perfect teacher, but always as a teacher who strives to learn and grow to be more caring; a teacher who makes mistakes, who has blind spots, who runs out of energy; who gets mad, sad, and glad; all in all, a human teacher. She did not recognize her own sexism, her subtle inequitable treatment of boys and girls, at first. It would have been easy to stop at her first theories which posited the *differences* in boy and girl dropouts entirely inside of the students, or as characteristics of gender and social class, without taking responsibility for her own differential treatment.

The beauty in this story, and the sensitivity it engenders, lies in its humanness. It is not a confessional, meant to ease her conscience, but a deep moral interrogation of her own teaching story. Beyond the message of the suffering caused by sexism in schools, is the story of a process of owning one's stories and taking moral responsibility as teachers. Based on her reflection, Johnson draws up a plan to recognize and involve her girls more and to spend more time with them. After listing several activities she concludes: "Of course, I'd continue to take the boys out too, just as I had always done, but from now on, the girls were at the top of my list and not the bottom."

STORYING MORAL PRACTICE; IDENTIFYING THE GOOD

Among other things, Sylvia Ashton-Warner (1963) is a theorist. Her theory, grounded in her work with children, is not the kind that is conducive to concise abstract description. Told in a language that borders on the poetic, she spins stories of school life in her "infant" room in New Zealand, where she teaches five-year-old Maori children how to read and write. Central to her thinking and theory making is the belief in what Ashton-Warner calls the *organic* life and a belief in the moral sovereignty of cultural varieties of this *inner* life. These concepts are developed and explored in her narratives. She offers no concise definitions, but spins multidimensional meanings into her stories. In Ashton-Warner's depiction, the organic life involves life energy, spirit, the inner being, and has two vents; creativity and destructiveness. This organic life involves an expression of culture, is "grown" *in* culture, and is unique as various cultures are unique. She believes reading and writing should evolve out of organic life and should contain words and symbols of cultural and personal significance to the child. Imposing words for reading and writing that do not involve the organic life, that do not involve the personal and cultural realities of the child works to stifle the child's creativity, leaving destructive acts as the avenue for venting the life energies of the organic self. These theories, values, and beliefs form the basis of Ashton-Warner's stories, moral stories about how we *should* engage children in expressions of symbolic process, how we *should* engage in practices of teaching. She tells a story about power.

> And how are you getting along with the Maoris? I asked a visiting teacher at our school.
> Oh, its the energy that's the trouble. They're always on the go. But once you have your foot on their neck they're all right.
> I understand . . . I understand. . . .
> I do. But I don't talk about it. I don't try to describe to others the force of the energy in our New Race. Indeed, when I speak of it as "force of energy" I'm grossly understating it. It's more like a volcano in continuous eruption. To stand on it, in my Maori infant room anyway, to stand on it with both feet and teach it in quiet orthodoxy would be a matter of murders and madnesses and spiritual death, while to teach it without standing on it is an utter impossibility. The only way I know of dealing with it is to let it teach itself. And that's what I've been forced to do. (pp. 90–91)

Ashton-Warner *protests* against imposing on children a curriculum that does not spring from their inner being. She cannot in good conscience put her foot on their necks to teach them words that have no life for them. However, throughout her writing we see the tension between meeting the expectations of those in authority, of doing things the way they have always been done, and following her own theories of the "good," based in her experience with children. Although the tension always exists in her stories, her choice and her values are clear.

> You've got to be either brave or desperate to take this road, even though in the end it leads to wide and happy fields. And I'm not brave. But I've got to the wide and happy fields. I'm all too aware that they are noisy fields, since my teacher's mind has been set by the past into the tradition of silence. But they're the only fields that I can understand and believe in, I being so simple—and even though the price is professional isolation and ineradicable, inescapable and corrosive guilt, here we stay. (p. 91)

Throughout her writing is the storying of this tension, the personal price one pays to "walk alone," and against the grain. Never quite able to free herself from the guilt of not meeting up to the traditional expectations, she stories her experience, her theories, her beliefs, in an effort to explain why she teaches differently, why her room is noisy, why her books look different, why her class looks different. She stories a version in which her practices make sense, constructing meanings as to what she should do. She describes her moral theories about control and power in the classroom.

> The spirit is so wild with the lid off. I'm still learning how to let it fly and still discipline it. It's got to be disciplined in a way that's hard to say. It still must have its range and its wing. . . . it must be free to dare the gale and sing, but its got to come home at the right time and nest in the right place. For the spirit to live its freest, the mind must acknowledge discipline. In this room anyway. In this room there is an outer discipline as well as an inner. They've got to listen to me when I speak and obey what I speak. I can only say that I don't often speak. And that I carefully weigh what I do speak. But the track between these two conditions, the spiritual freedom and the outer discipline, is narrower than any tightrope, and seldom can I say that I have walked it. (p. 92)

In this paragraph, Ashton-Warner stories another tension, the tension between spiritual freedom, freedom of the organic life to grow, to express, to create, and an outer discipline, establishing an order that will secure a place conducive for that creativity to emerge. This is not a tension that she claims to resolve, but a force within the context of teaching that she must always grapple with, trying to find a balance. Her ideal balance, while not free from the issues of discipline and control, is founded on the values of cherishing the "organic spirit" within the child first and foremost. This requires her to forsake uncritical traditional theories and practices, unspoken rules of "orderly" classrooms and unspoken assumptions that measure teachers' successes by such things as the noise levels in their classes.

> The volcanic energy, precipitated from the combustion of the old race and the young, the volcanic energy of the new race blows—but is directed. It was exhausting at first, this controlling of the direction of the blasts; and not without risks, this changing of the vents, for the young Maori warriors are full of "take, break, fight, and be first" when they come; but it is not as exhausting or as dangerous as standing in the way of it. Sometimes when a tribal excitement surges through the school, the tidal emotion rises up to the level of our eyes and over our signposts so that we think as we drown, "the foot on the neck." (pp. 92–93)

Delving deeper into the issue of control, Ashton-Warner theorizes about the source of the incredible energy of "the new race." She sees the source of this energy in the combining of races that forms a "combustion." And when these forces, born in community, in culture, surge through the school, she locates the temptations to contain and control that energy in the fear of being overwhelmed by it. Although she understands this reaction, she stories theories of a different route, what she believes to be a more moral route, which channels that volcanic energy into creative expression and learning.

> But I know that there is too much material and too much drive in the wake of these floods, so we hold our breath and rely on the inner disciplines. At least it's life. For both them and me. And the creative work that comes from it, especially the books, is something I'd pay anything for. (1963, p. 93)

Identifying her valuing in the creative process, she swings back to assure her readers once again that this does not mean that anything goes. Rather, she promotes an inner order that allows for and celebrates the emergence of the organic life. She has a passion for this life, a love for this life, and it is this love and passion that fuels theory and practice.

> Yet, I'm a disciplinarian. It's just that I like the lid off. I like seeing what's there. I like unpredictability and gaiety and interesting people, however small, and funny things happening and wild things happening and sweet, and everything that life is, uncovered. I hate covers of any kind. I like the true form of living, even in school. I'm in love with the organic shape. (p. 93)

Bringing us back full circle, Ashton-Warner protests the practice of "the foot on the neck" and fashions a moral theory of what comprises better practice.

> "They're all right once you've got your foot on their neck."
> I understand. I understand. But communication and creativity are abler teachers than a foot. (p. 93)

By storying her theory, Ashton-Warner is able to accommodate the paradox of being teacher and disciplinarian that teachers struggle with so often. She can theorize about schooling within the context of the institution which expects something different of her than she is willing to give. She stories her experiences in an attempt to explain the moral merits of her choices.

STORYING ORDER

Much like Sylvia Ashton-Warner, George Dennison (1969) tells stories about teaching which situates his experiences at The First Street School within a theoretical dialogue about what should happen in schools. He ties his theorizing about education into his own teaching experiences, but also connects those experiences and theories to other theories and stories about education. He theorizes how school experiences are structured and stories the different possibilities he enjoys at the small experimental school in which he works. He compares this context to a rendition of a traditional bureaucratic school, drawing connections between these contexts and the types of relationships and experiences of schooling that are possible in each. One thing Dennison shows us is what can happen in the name of education when it occurs within a context that does not use knowledge as control.

Dennison is very interested in the implications of power and control in schooling. In one story he describes an incident in which two warring factions within his small classroom determine to settle their differences with fists. He masterfully stories a version of order and control that runs contrary to moral canons of education that color student fighting as *bad* and teacher control as *good*. Rather than to blindly apply meanings that had been handed down to him to understand his students' behavior, he watches his students with an eye to what their fighting means to them and what they accomplish by it. He opens himself to their meanings, and allows himself to see beauty in their ways.

Dennison frames the story by describing his theory concerning the detrimental effect he believes teachers' attempts to control violence have on their students. He describes a theory that runs counter to popular notions of "common sense."

> I am convinced that when children (except perhaps for the seriously disturbed ones) remain vicious or violent toward each other, it is because their motives are invaded by those of adults, and they cannot evolve their own better terms of relations. When they're given enough room, their adjustments to each other, and to their own fears and impulses, are marvelously creative and subtle. (1969, p. 137)

Once his moral stance is made explicit, Dennison goes on to tell a story which exemplifies that stance. Notice how this stance is illustrated in his relationship to his students. We do not see Dennision trying to curtail their actions, but rather respect the request of the student to not "break it up."

> Yesterday, some trivial incident occurred, and the boys decided to "fight it out." At first the fight was scheduled to take place after school, but then they decided to have it in the gym. They ran down the stairs in a flock, Vicente looking back at me and raising his finger: "Don't you break it up, Man!" (p. 138)

As he describes the fight and the preliminary arrangements the boys made beforehand, he contructs stories and interprets them simultaneously. He describes the students' actions as *cooperative,* bestowing on them a moral virtue usually not associated with fighting. He uses narrative, much as Bruner explains its function, "to find an intentional state that mitigates or at least makes comprehensible a deviation from a canonical cultural pattern." (Dennison, 1969, p. 49). His interpretation of the students' behavior, based on what he imagines as, and stories as, their intentions, makes Dennison's behavior, his lack of intervention, morally comprehensible and defensible.

> The boys shouted back and forth excitedly—insults, plans for the fight, threats, boasts, and some kind of cooperative exchange concerning vague outer limits of behavior. They cooperated, too, in getting out the mats and laying them in a great square. I helped them with this and then withdrew to the end of the gym where I sat on the floor and leaned against the wall.
>
> A great shout went up, a roar, and all five piled into each other . . . and stopped abruptly to let Jose take off his shirt. Stanley and Willard took their shirts off, too. They were about to clash again when Stanley paused and took off his shoes, and so Willard and Jose took their shoes off, too. The roar went up again and they tangled, Stanley and Willard against Jose, Julio, and Vicente. (pp. 138–139)

Once he has established the fight as having subtle moral dimensions, he goes on to interpret ways in which the fight functions to bring the boys together.

> There was much cursing, many shouts of pain—strange shouts, really, for each one had in it a tinge of protest and flattery. It was in these overtones that one could sense the fine changes in their relations. They were saying things for which they had no words, and the refinement of this communication was extraordinary and beautiful. (p. 139)

Painting their fight as "extraordinary and beautiful," Dennison maps a different moral meaning onto a school fight than what is expected—a particular version of fighting that counters a deeply ingrained notion that fighting is always *bad* and it is the *teacher's responsibility* to prevent fights whenever possible and punish fighters to teach students a moral lesson about violence. What we see in its place is a morality similar to Ashton-Warner's—an inherent valuing of the students' interactions and intentions and of their ability to regulate their own behavior.

It was immediately apparent that the boys had set some kind of limit to their violence, though they had not spoken of limits. Rules, codes, acknowledgments popped
up spontaneously and changed swiftly. When anyone got hurt, he stepped off the
mats (it was usually Julio, holding his head and complaining in a voice which paid
tribute to Willard's strength); and the rule was accepted by all, without having been
announced, that no one could be attacked when he stepped off the mat. (p. 139)

Dennison stories a process in which students come to appreciate one another. He
is able to story a moral theory, which might not fly without his contextualized
interpretation. He is so convincing in his storying that when he describes
"punches as compliments" we are able to accept this seemingly paradoxical statement without flinching.

Occasionally, as the boys rolled and squirmed, they also punched each other in the
ribs. These blows, however, were almost formal and were very subtly adjusted. The
loser must prove that he is really struggling, and so in order to ensure himself against
the contempt of the victor, he punches him in the ribs. Delivered with just the right
force, these punches remain compliments ("I esteem you and want you to think well
of me"). They are tributes, too, to the reality of the fight. Delivered a bit harder, they
are "unfair." Delivered still harder, they precipitate a bloodletting. And so they are
very nicely attuned. (p. 140)

Dennison describes the outcome of the fight as a sort of magic, a transformation
that occurs in the boys' relationship. His story takes us to a new place of possibility, not one so foreign that we don't understand it, but one somehow familiar, one
that resonates with something we already "know" from our experience, something
about human dignity and goodness.

Now all the boys come to the mats and round things off with a general melee. Jose
is somewhat abashed by his defeat, but he squares off against Willard, bluffing to the
hilt and acting tough. He takes a boxer's stance, with curled fingers and weaving
shoulders, saying, "Come on, man, come on." Willard looks at him for a moment. In
boxing he could demolish Jose, and there is no doubt about it. Nothing shows in his
smile. He puts up his hands and shadowboxes with Jose. In fact, they are playing
together, and this is the first time. (p. 142)

Few teachers would have the freedom to see the beauty in a school fight. Rather,
we might be too concerned about liability, our own reputation as teachers, or
believe that our own sense of moral indignation at violence was based on a universal ethic. Or we might recognize subtle dimensions of moral behavior in the
fight, but lack time or storytelling ability to nestle those meanings into narratives
that situate them differently.

It is easy to see that another teacher, with different beliefs, might story this fight
very differently. The same clay of common experience might be modeled into a

story that situated the meanings for the fight in the students' race and social class, or attributed it to "emotional disturbance," or the failure of teachers and parents to instill moral values in today's youth. Dennison's rendition of the school fight was not meant to be used to establish a new moral imperative. He does not try to convince us that all school fights are stories of cooperation and transformation, only that sometimes they can be. Reading Dennison's story might inspire teachers to be more open to the experiences in our classrooms; to try to see order in disorder. It may help us hesitate before we blindly impose meaning onto events. It may make us more sensitive to and interested in our students' meanings, or it may allow us to trust our own valuing even when it runs contrary to long-held beliefs.

TEACHERS' STORIES OF SYSTEMS

If there is a central theme that emerges in this book, it is that teachers have a tremendous amount of power to do both harm and good. With all this power, why do teachers so often feel powerless? Iris Young (1990) attributes this paradox to the characteristics of bureaucracy. She tells us that in bureaucracies it is possible to have power over others' behavior while not having power over one's own behavior. In this scheme, teachers are seen as *agents* of the system's power. According to Spence (1978, 1980), this configuration of top-down power, an inherent condition of hierarchy, is promoted through an unspoken ethic of conformity. He makes a convincing argument that hierarchical organizations work against individuals taking moral responsibility for their own actions by positing moral authority above them. Premised on the privileging of "expert knowledge," teachers are often expected to promote the moral authority of the institution over their own personal moral stories and those of their students.

One can easily imagine the types of responses a teacher like Dennison might have gotten in a more traditional school for allowing the fight. "What, you let them fight and thought it was beautiful?" The administrator might ask before s/he launched into a moral lesson about liability and the teacher's responsibility to students and institution to maintain order in the school. Without the benefit of his beautifully crafted story, a teacher like Dennison would most likely be scrambling to justify his own actions to an administrator who did not have the benefit of seeing the beauty in it for him or herself.

Teachers who story their experiences are able to construct moral meanings within the context of their relationships with students and administrators within an educational organization. In addition to storying their experiences with students, the above teacher-authors also story their relationship to the "system" and how their own connected ways of knowing and being are often discounted along with those of their students. They story their experiences upward in the hierarchy too, toward sources of power that attempt to constrain their knowing to predetermined truths and roles. They use their stories to effectively bring unspoken rules and assumptions to consciousness and to question the morality of educational practices. Each of these three teachers who so carefully story respect for the dignity of their students' meanings, story very different meanings when they speak of the power of the "system."

Johnson (1995) describes a conversation with an administrator which occurs after the two have a disagreement about how to handle a potentially dangerous situation with a student. Johnson is frustrated by the lack of concern and action shown by the administrator. Located in a relationship in which roles are unequal and narrowly defined, she stories the threats which are intended to keep her "in line."

> "How long have you been teaching here, Miss Johnson?
> "Three years."
> "You may be granted tenure this year, then. Is that right?"
> I didn't bother to answer because it wasn't really a question. It was a reminder that Mr. Simms was in charge of the committee that would evaluate my performance and decide whether to grant tenure.
> "I honestly do appreciate your concern about your students, Miss Johnson," Mr. Simms said, in a thin, tired voice, and for once I believed him. "But you have many more students to worry about. I told you I would take care of this matter, and I will. That's my job. Your job is to teach. Period. If you interfere with my job, you won't have a job to worry about. And if you aren't here, you won't be able to help any of those students that you love so much." (p. 164)

Throughout her story, Ashton-Warner (1963) describes her conflicts with those in authority in the system. She struggles with her work not being recognized as legitimate. She struggles with not looking good to others. The two paragraphs written below occur one after the other in her story. She leaves us to make the connections between feeling singled out as a "bad" teacher and her decision to leave teaching. Her discouragement rings clear in her writing.

> We had our grading this week. The men were well marked. Tom and K., but as usual I was very low. There is no doubt about it. I am a very low-ability teacher. My sister Daphne says on this matter that it would be a disgrace for a woman in my position to be a good teacher. As for myself, maybe it is a distinction of some kind to be unacceptable in New Zealand teaching. I walk alone, like Edmund Burke. We are "rogues," the term critics give to people they can't classify. That's the alternative assumption. I use both.
> Saturday morning. I have come to a decision this morning. I'm resigning at the end of this year. I have established, begun so much here. Everything of myself. I have put it in here. But I'm going to leave it. I've had enough. (p. 103)

Dennison (1969) sums up his feelings about the devastating effects of "the system" in few brief sentences. He tells us:

> The present quagmire of public education is entirely the result of unworkable cen-
> tralization and the lust for control that permeates every bureaucratic institution. (p. 13)

Each of these teacher-authors storied versions of school life that align the system with the *bad*. Their stories provide contextualized renditions of the tensions
that result from their attempts to respect the integrity of their students' ways of
knowing and being, within an institution that does not afford the teachers nor students the same respect.

Pressures of socialization within educational contexts can be strong (Zeichner
& Gore, 1990). The pressure is increased by the fear of the loss of one's position
if conformity is not maintained. The philosophy of "go along to get along" is easy
to adopt under such pressure. Spence (1980) tells us that in a hierarchy, the people
who make the decisions are not the ones who are in a position to know what must
be done, they are removed from the work. The teacher, in a position between the
students and the administration, is pulled as the demands of the system and the
needs of the students become more divergent. Very often teachers in this type of
situation talk of acting as buffers between their students and the system.

One of the most powerful ways to address and counteract the distancing
between the system's vision and the teacher's vision is through the sharing of stories. Administrators who pressure teachers to participate in educational practices
which teachers do not believe are in the best interest of their students, often make
these decisions without an adequate understanding of the students' and teacher's
needs. Stories that help administrators understand can bridge the gaps between
those who make the decisions and those who are most affected by them. It is likewise important that teachers listen to administrators' stories as well and try to
understand their perspectives. Although administrators are often not in a position
to understand classroom needs as well as the teacher, teachers are rarely in a
position to grasp the broader system's perspective of the administrator.

It is helpful when teachers have opportunities to develop the ability to take on
multiple perspectives in relationship to problem solving and working with others.
If a teacher is able to understand the points of view of those around him or her
(other teachers, administrators, parents, and students), then s/he is in a better position to work with these individuals in groups. Understanding a point of view does
not necessitate condoning it or agreeing with it, it simply provides a point of reference and a starting place to begin dialogue. It is through listening to others' stories, that we can begin to see from their perspectives.

It is also important for teachers to develop a personal and professional support
system of colleagues, friends, and family members. Teachers need to be able to
share their stories and their visions within a safe context of like-minded souls. A
teacher without a support system often feels isolated and can easily begin to doubt
his/her practices and vision when challenges are encountered.

Many schools and districts provide opportunities for teachers to participate in
decision making. Teachers can foster reform through their involvement in

site-based management, professional organizations, and learning communities. These types of groups create spaces for teachers to have voice in decisions that impact their classrooms and promote collegial professional growth. It is important that teachers enter into decision making processes when they have opportunities to do so.

Teachers need to be persistent in order to navigate the system with determination and finesse. They must learn to pick their battles wisely, and realize that if they become alienated within the system that their students may be alienated too. With time, teachers begin to recognize, within their individual contexts, when a policy or directive is not worth the emotional or professional cost to confront it. In such cases, they need to find creative ways to navigate around the directive while still maintaining their place within the system and protecting their vision of care.

CONCLUSION

Teachers' stories allow them to construct meanings in relationship to experience, theory, and social and political structures. Teachers are able to fashion not only stories of schooling, but interpretations also. This storying is an act of power which helps to redirect the flow of power in a hierarchy, allowing the determination of moral goodness to emerge from experience and relationship, from the lives of students and teachers, from the meanings of culture and personal history.

As we read stories about schooling, we are able to access how education makes us feel about ourselves and others. We are able to identify what hurts and what helps along the way. We are able to move into a place of author-ity from whence we can begin to re-imagine education in more caring and ethical ways. We each have our own stories, our own histories within educational institutions. Reading others' stories allows us frameworks to interrogate our own stories.

Story is a powerful means of transformation. What we may enter into as a source of comfort and entertainment may land us in very different waters indeed. If we are not careful, story may lure us into the ranks of educational reformers. We may find ourselves telling our own stories, constructing theories, identifying the moral *good* as well as the *bad*. We may find ourselves veering to those lonely places outside of the educational mainstream. It is not an easy journey, but for those who are willing to follow their heart and soul into moral realms of education--story can take us there.

REFERENCES

Ashton-Warner, S. (1963). *Teacher*. New York: Simon & Shuster.
Ayers, W. (1992). Teachers' stories: Autobiography and inquiry. In E. W. Ross, J. Cornett, & G. McCutcheon (Eds.), *Teacher personal theorizing: Connecting curriculum,*

practice, theory, and research (pp. 35–52). Albany: State University of New York Press.

Bruner, J. (1990). *Acts of meanng.* Cambridge: Harvard University Press.

Cochran-Smith, M., & Lytle, S. (1993). *Inside/outside: teacher research and knowledge.* New York: Teachers College Press.

Cooper, J. E. (1991). Telling our own stories: The reading and writing of journals and diaries. In C. Witherall & N. Noddings (Eds.), *Stories lives tell: Narrative and dialogue in education* (pp. 96–112). New York: Teachers College Press.

Dennison, G. (1969). *The lives of children: The story of the first street school.* New York: Random House.

Eagleton, T. (1983). *Literary theory: An introduction.* Minneapolis: University of Minnesota Press.

Fine, M. (1994). Distance and other stances: Negotiations of power inside feminist research. In A. Gitlin (Ed.), *Power and method: Political activism and educational research* (pp. 13–35). New York: Routledge.

Foster, M. (1994). The power to one thing is never the power to know all things: Methodological notes on two studies of black American teachers. In A. Gitlin (Ed.), *Power and method: Political activism and educational research.* New York: Routledge.

Gitlin, A., & Russell, R. (1994). Alternative methodologies and the research context. In A. Gitlin (Ed.), *Power and method: Political activism and educational research* (pp. 181–202). New York: Routledge.

Gitlin, A., Bringhurst, K., Burns, M., Cooley, V., Myers, B., Price, K., Russell, R., & Tiess, P. (1992). *Teachers' voices for school change: An introduction to educative research.* New York: Teachers College Press.

Griffith, M. (1995). (Auto)biography and epistemology. *Educational Review, 47*(1), 75–88.

Helle, A. P. (1991). Reading women's autobiographies: A map of reconstructed knowing. In C. Witherall & N. Noddings (Eds.), *Stories lives tell: Narrative and dialogue in education* (pp. 48–66). New York: Teachers College Press.

Isenberg, J. (1994). *Going by the book.* Westport CT: Bergin & Garvey.

Johnson, L. (1995). *Girls at the back of the class.* New York: St. Martin's Press.

Kincheloe, J. (1991). *Teachers as researchers: Qualitative inquiry as a path to empowerment.* Bristol, PA: Falmer Press.

Lather, P. (1994). Fertile obsession: Validity after poststructuralism. In A. Gitlin (Ed.),*Power and method: Political activism and educational research* (pp. 36–60). New York: Routledge.

Leck, G. M. (1994). Queer relations with educational research. In A. Gitlin (Ed.), *Power and method: Political activism and educational research* (pp. 77–96). New York: Routledge.

McLaren, P. (1989). *Life in schools.* White Plains, NY: Longman.

Morris, J. (1995). Personal and political: A feminist perspective on researching disability. In J. Holland & M. Blair (Eds.), *Debates and issues in feminist research and pedagogy* (pp. 262–271). Philadelphia: The Open University.

Noddings, N. (1991). Stories in dialogue: Caring and interpersonal relationships. In C. Witherell & N. Noddings (Eds.), *Stories lives tell: Narrative and dialague in education* (pp. 157–170). New York: Teachers Colege Press.

Spence, L. (1978). *The politics of social knowledge.* University Park: The Pennsylvania State University Press.

Spence, L. (1980). Moral judgment and bureaucracy. In R. W. Wilson & G. J. Schochnet (Eds.), *Moral development and politics* (pp. 137–168). New York: Praeger.

Stanley, L. (Ed.). (1990). *Feminist praxis: Research, theory and epistemology in feminist sociology*. London: Routledge.

Stone, L. (1992). Philosophy, meaning constructs and teacher theorizing. In E. W. Ross, J. Cornett, & G. McCutcheon (Eds.), *Teacher personal theorizing: Connecting curriculum, practice, theory, and research* (pp. 19–34). Albany: State University of New York Press.

Tappan, M. B., & Brown, L. M. (1991). Stories told and lessons learned: Toward a narrative approach to moral development and moral education. In C. Witherall & N. Noddings (Eds.), *Stories lives tell: Narrative and dialogue in education* (pp. 171–192). New York: Teachers College Press.

Taylor, C. (1989). *Sources of the self*. Cambridge: Harvard University Press.

Tierney, W. G. (1994). On method and hope. In A. Gitlin (Ed.), *Power and method: Political activism and educational research*. New York: Routledge.

Weber, S., & Mitchell, C. (1995). *That's funny, you don't look like a teacher!* Washington, D.C: Falmer Press.

Young, I. M. (1990). *Justice and the politics of difference*. Princeton, NJ: Princeton University Press.

Witherell, C. (1991). The self in narrative: A journey into paradox. In C. Witherell & N. Noddings (Eds.), *Stories Lives Tell: Narrative and Dialogue in Education*. New York: Teachers College Press.

Zeichner, K., & Gore, J. (1990). Teacher socialization. In. R. Houston (Ed.), *Handbook of Research on Teacher Education* (pp. 329–348). New York: Macmillan.

8

ETHICS, POLITICS, AND THE UNINTENDED CRUELTIES OF TEACHING

Terry Jo Smith
National-Louis University

Scot Danforth
University of Missouri–St. Louis

In this book the various authors have written stories and theories which somehow address the powerful spaces between teachers and students. We have entered those spaces through students writing lovingly about their teachers and teachers writing lovingly about their students. We have moved into more threatening waters and looked at the ways in which teachers in our pasts have hurt us. We have looked at pedagogy in an attempt to uncover hidden cruelty in practice and policy, and we have reflected on ethical deliberation as a means to purposefully engage in just decision making processes. We have walked around this relational space between teachers and students, created it and recreated from many different subject positions and through many different theoretical lenses.

In this chapter we enter into this space from a position that is perhaps the most vulnerable and threatening perspective of all, as teachers look at the ways in which they have been cruel or hurtful toward students. This perilous journey is worth the risk as it has the potential to move us from a place of hurting to healing, from a place of fear to courage. Critically examining our own teaching is a potentially transformative act of caring, as it takes a caring teacher to be willing to look at the ways s/he has been cruel. It is difficult enough to look at the pain we have suffered at the hands of others, but to look at the pain we have caused others takes us into a most guarded and disturbing place. Yet, this is a personally powerful place and by engaging in honest self-reflection we can begin to take conscious responsibility for the unintended and often unacknowledged ways we have hurt others.

LETTERS THAT ARE SENT

During my career as a teacher, I (the first author) have received many notes, letters, and student reflection papers which have thanked me for being a caring teacher. These never fail to encourage me and fill me with joy at my choice of vocation. I have kept many of these letters as treasures and testaments of what I value most in teaching. However, there is one letter that stands out among all the rest. The letter came to my attention again years after it was written as I was going through a folder of my former students' writing. As I reread their stories and essays, I was filled with sentimental feelings and a sense of missing the students who had touched my life in profound and beautiful ways. Totally lost in remembrance, I came across a paper folded up with my name on front. I was jolted from my blissful reminiscence when I read the following letter:

Dear Ms. Smith,

I am tired of being in the EH [Emotionally Handicapped] program. You say I should be more like the other EH kids. But I don't know how. I have drifted so far away. They make fun of how I dress, but they don't stop to think that I am growing and my clothes are shrinking. You say I should have a better attitude.

Ms. Smith, you are right, I have a problem. I don't know how to solve it. I need help and I just don't know how to get help. I feel lost. I hoped you could help me, but I know you don't want to hear my self-pity.

Your student,
Randy

A flood of guilt surged through me as I read this letter and remembered Randy. He was very perceptive; I had not wanted to hear his self-pity. Randy was a student I really didn't like and it was obvious from his note that he knew it on some level. I was not alone. Randy wasn't liked by anyone I knew, teacher or student. That made it worse. There was no one for him to turn to, as he stated so clearly in his letter.

What does a teacher do with this kind of letter? What does a teacher do when she realizes the limits of her caring? Even as I write this I want to assure readers that I was, in most cases, a very caring teacher. I want to type in other letters telling of how I was loved and appreciated for going way beyond the call of duty to help my students. I want to describe details about Randy that will make you understand why he was so difficult to care for. I want to defend myself against judgment: yours and mine. But that would not help me become a more caring teacher.

As I read the letter from Randy, I had to admit that I did not always act in caring ways toward Randy, though I sincerely tried, in spite of strong feelings of aversion I felt toward him. I didn't like being in his presence. Most of my students had experienced this type of aversion more than once in school. They were all labeled emotionally handicapped and were set off in pre-fabricated buildings (portables) at the far edge of the school property. More times than I could count general education teachers would sincerely ask me how I could stand to work with "those" kids. I was always offended by these comments. I told anyone who asked that they were great kids and I loved working with them. Except for one. Randy was a child who was the outcast in group of outcasts. He had no place to be, no one to turn to.

Randy's letter clearly states the depth of his aloneness and despair. I could feel this coming from Randy, but it was difficult to find a place in me from which to respond to his sadness. To me, Randy seemed too needy, too wimpy. He was 16, but looked and acted 10. He was everything I had been raised, in my working-class background, to believe was unattractive in a boy. I was much more drawn to the street kids I worked with, who had been taught to keep a tough exterior. I, too, had been raised to keep a stiff upper lip. Perhaps I could not tolerate in Randy, what was not tolerated in me. Perhaps Randy made me afraid of encountering the disowned parts of myself that have been neatly hidden away. If nothing else, the letter from Randy has helped me to realize that when I think and write about cruelty in the classroom, I am not writing about someone else. I am not above the conversation.

COMPLEXITY OF SCHOOL RELATIONSHIPS

Throughout this book we have looked at care and cruelty in schools, and we have conveniently dichotomized these constructs as we located them in separate practices and separate people. We have written about caring teachers and cruel teachers, caring practices and negative practices, in ways that could be interpreted as if these never occupied the same person or place. We have also characterized practices and interactions in ways that could be interpreted as clearly either good or bad. However, within the complex web of relationships there are often paradoxical and conflicting layers and levels of meaning.

An example of the complexity of classroom relationships may be seen with the case of a teacher who is very protective of her students. This may impart to them the undying concern she has for them as she struggles to protect them from others in the school or the world beyond school. This can be experienced by the students as caring, and probably remembered lovingly. Students may feel safer and more secure in their classroom, knowing that their teacher will go to bat for them if the need arises. This may allow them to relax more and focus on their learning. And yet, if this teacher doesn't teach students to be self-advocates, or engenders in them a dependence on her, or requires from them unending gratitude for her sacrifices, she may cause them harm at another, less conscious, level. Students may sense, but not be able to put their finger on, the teacher's underlying belief that they are not capable of fending for themselves.

An opposite dynamic can also occur. A teacher who believes her students are very capable may expect a tremendous amount from them. At times she may be perceived by students as asking too much. However, when students grow in confidence and competence due to their classroom challenges they often come to understand the care involved in setting high expectations. Or it may not be until these students have children or students of their own that they begin to understand how much easier it is to ask less versus the amount of work and love involved in pushing students to reach higher. These more subtle layers aren't as easily detected, verbalized, or recognized, but they impact students deeply nonetheless.

In addition to the complexity of layers of relationship between teachers and individual students, the fact that these relationships occur in groups that have similar characteristics to families complicates interactions even further. Often a teacher may be drawn to a student who is experiencing a lot of personal difficulties and react with added attention and support. In the case of this particular child, this is a caring response. However, because the teacher's time is a limited resource, other students may feel jealous or slighted by the teacher's increased attention to the other student. With or without benefit of the knowledge of the first student's situation, others may feel jealous and resentful. This may play out in negative attempts to get the teacher's attention or withdrawal from what feels like a painful place. The experience of care and cruelty exists in a complex web of interactions, not simply in intentions and actions of individuals.

It is important that we adopt an understanding about the complexity of the demands of teaching which allows us room to look at ourselves as teachers and recognize the enormous difficulty of this job. We have cultural images and stereotypes of the saintly teacher, the person who never makes a mistake, who is always kind and giving, who is always accessible to her students, who always likes everyone, and who has an endless source of energy and commitment. This myth is perpetuated in teacher education programs and by texts that do not address the more human dimensions of teacher–student relationships, but assume that if one uses certain methods and integrated curricula that all students will learn and flourish.

I can remember a significant turning point in my teaching career in this regard. It was during my third year of teaching middle school. I was usually a very patient teacher, who allowed my students to work through their difficulties in the classroom rather than sending them home or to the principal's office. My students came to count on that. One day a boy came in cursing and very upset. I usually allowed the kids to blow off steam, then helped them work out solutions to their problems. This particular day, I just snapped and ordered him to go home. I sent my teacher's aide to call his mother. At this, the student really lost control and ended up trashing another teacher's room and getting arrested.

I felt terrible. I knew I had provoked him with my uncharacteristic impatience and quick move to send him home. I went to speak to the assistant principal, who I counted on for advice, support, and friendship. I sat in his office, filled with guilt and remorse. I had worked so long and hard with this student and I had let him down. Now he was suspended for 10 days. The assistant principal listened patiently and when I had exhausted my confession, asked me how many decisions I made in a day.

"I don't know, maybe a hundred," I said.

"Do you expect you'll never make a mistake?" he asked.

He helped me see that I was very rough on myself, that I allowed kids many mistakes and many chances, but expected I would always know the right thing to do and always do it. He told me I needed to be easier on myself, to give myself some of the same room I gave my students to be human. It had never occurred to me until that point that I had completely unrealistic expectations for myself. However, realizing that of course I would make some mistakes did not provide an excuse for me to be a cruel teacher, but it opened up a space in which I could examine my own teaching without being shut down by fear and guilt.

Sometimes teachers go through very difficult times in their school and personal lives. During the break-up of a significant relationship, the illness of a loved one, or the loss of a family member or friend, for example, teachers may find themselves with very limited patience, focus, or endurance in the classroom. Very caring teachers can go through difficult times in which they may not have the same emotional resources of care and patience that they usually possess. The more honest teachers can be about their own limitations in such times, the more they can allow their students to care for them when they experience difficulty. Caring is healing for those who give it as well as receive it. Teachers who allow their students to care for them during their own difficult times allow their students opportunities to learn and grow.

In the situation described above where I was impatient with my student, I opened the door to healing by caring for myself, by forgiving myself for my very human shortcomings. Once I realized I had made a mistake, not because I was a terrible person but a human one, I was able to call this student and his mother and talk with them. I took the student out for lunch the following day and apologized for being so abrupt and impatient. The interesting thing was that this student, who had been so furious with me and hurt by my insensitivity, admitted his own contribution to the previous day's events. I think when we create a space in which can be imperfect without feeling overwhelmed with guilt and shame, we invite our students to do the same. This opens the space for growth and understanding.

THE ROLE OF FEAR

Fear is at the root of many of the cruel acts that occur in schools and in the world beyond schools. In his recent book *The Courage to Teach,* Parker Palmer (1998) explores how fear invades educational contexts at every level. One of the major premises Palmer bases this work on is the notion that we have paid a lot of attention in educational discourse to what is taught, how it is taught, and occasionally why something is taught, but rarely do we speak about the self who teaches. Palmer journeys into the interiors of his own teaching self as a means to illuminate these often negated and neglected inner landscapes of teaching. What he finds when he journeys inward is a self who cares very much about his students and the quality of his teaching, but who is, even after years of successful practice, often very afraid. Palmer sums up what he thinks is often at the base of our fear:

> We collaborate with the structures of separation because they promise to protect us against one of the deepest fears at the heart of being human—the fear of having a live encounter with alien "otherness," whether the other is a student, a colleague, a subject, or a self-dissenting voice within. We fear encounters in which the other is free to be itself, to speak its own truth, to tell us what we may not wish to hear. We want those encounters on our own terms, so we can control their outcomes, so they will not threaten our view of world or self. (p. 37)

Palmer goes on to say that the fear of the live encounter is comprised of a whole series of fears that begins in a fear of diversity. When we acknowledge that there are many diverse perspectives and ways of making sense of the world, we have to acknowledge that our view is just that, a view. It means we would have to consider others' views as legitimate, and that may even challenge us to have to change how we live.

Educational structures, theory, and conventional teaching practices allow teachers a ready escape from facing these fears. We can teach from a place of authority in which we hold ourselves, our knowledge, and our perspective above question. Many of us have encountered the teacher who is *never* wrong. While these teachers may arouse fear in students, Palmer makes it clear that this type of teacher is often motivated by fear him- or herself. The following excerpt from the novel *Crackpot,* by Adele Wiseman (1993) conjures up a vivid image of a teacher's inner fear which resonates on many levels with Palmer's theorizing.

> Hoda's feeling about her new teacher's attitude to Morgan came very close to the truth. Had the children had the daring to put their stray intuitions into words they might have realized, as some of them vaguely apprehended at times, that Miss Bolt-holmsup was afraid of them. . . . Like all who live in constant danger, Miss Bolt-holmsup in her cage was always alert, interpreting signs, picking up motions, working out new tactics, forestalling, soothing, guarding, doubling back, retreating, making plans, keeping them busy, keeping them diverted, above all keeping them

under control. She was, in fact, considered by a respectful principal, to be the hardest working teacher in his school. . . . For Miss Boltholmsup was plagued, in particular, by the animal natures of her charges. "They mature so much more quickly in this district. It's where they come from, those backward places," she confided, occasionally to one of her few friends. . . . The burden of knowledge was hers and hers alone, and it wore her out, wore her out with the strain of seeing and having, perforce, to pay no attention: wore her out with simply the effort she put in daily to avert the undefined disasters with which their presence fill her life. (p. 90–91)

In this account we see the fear of the live encounter with the Other as it is translated into educational practices that work to constrain authentic relationship, that structure the space between teacher and students in ways in which students' selves are discouraged from emerging. These practices, like those discussed by Colucci in Chapter 3, are cruel in ways that are difficult to articulate or pin down as they may be encountered in the midst of soothing words, and constant diversions from how it really feels to be in the classroom.

In the following excerpt from *This Rough Magic,* by Daniel Lindley (1993), we are privy to a teachers' thoughts and fears as he tries to make sense of his students' behaviors.

One day about three weeks after I'd started, I was teaching one of my more difficult classes (but not the zoo) when, with no warning the whole class applauded. Nothing like this had happened to me before. I was startled and certainly threatened. I thought they'd met before class and conspired to do it: Let's give Lindley the applause treatment, I imaged them saying, and then plotting a time. I put on my severest voice, which wasn't very severe, and demanded to know what was going on. Silence. I demanded again. Silence, and lots of looking down, or at least looking away from me. I demanded again, less urgently. A hand twitched into the air and went right back down, but I'd seen it and I called on its owner. She looked at me shyly. "Mr. Lindley, we clapped because you smiled." (p. 10)

As students, many of us have experienced the teacher who does not smile, who brings little of the joy of learning into the classroom that would entice us to follow in his or her footsteps. But it is rare, indeed, to be invited into the personal world of such a teacher. More often, students encounter the teacher's persona; the masks, the role, and the professional distance, which act as barriers to entering into shared space, the space where both teachers and students can teach and learn.

We see in Lindley's brief autobiographical snippet, the reversal of our traditional images of the knowing teacher and unknowing students. The teacher is the one who is "in the dark," confused by his students' behavior, unable to see beyond his own defenses and to reflect on his own behavior. From his place of fear, he imagines a conspiracy, a plot against him, and he attempts to conjure up the persona of a teacher, an adult, an authority, a threat. However, when the truth comes out, it is his own awkward distancing from his students which is at the source of their seemingly *alien* behavior.

FEAR OF REPRISALS AND HARSH JUDGMENTS

One of the focuses of teachers' stories examined in the previous chapter involved teachers storying their feelings about the school systems in which they worked. Often, teachers feel intimidated by the demands of the system and feel afraid to question policies and practices that they may not feel are in the best interests of students. They may want to interact with students in ways that are more respectful of students' individual differences, but feel compelled to fit in with the directives of the administration and/or the school climate.

Alice Miller (1990), whose work we have looked at extensively in Chapter 1, suggests that even as adults, many people act like frightened children in relationship to authority figures. This is particularly true, according to Miller, for people who were not permitted to speak their minds and hearts as children.

> If an adult has not developed a mind of his own, then he will find himself at the mercy of the authorities for better or worse, just as an infant finds itself at the mercy of its parents. Saying no to those more powerful will always seem too threatening to him. (p. 84)

Even very assertive teachers, who are quite comfortable speaking their minds, are often silenced by their fear of losing their jobs, being transferred, not receiving tenure, being treated as outcasts, or simply laughed at within schools. Often teachers are aware that the policies in schools are unfair, cruel, or prejudicial, but they lack the courage to speak up.

Herbert Kohl (1994), in his essay on creative maladjustment focuses on ways for teachers to become creatively maladjusted to the absurdity and cruelty present in many systems. Kohl recognizes fear as a central ingredient in maintaining systems that do not address the needs of all students. He suggests that teachers need to find creative ways to become maladjusted to oppressive systems, rather than giving up. He writes:

> When it is impossible to remain in harmony with one's environment without giving up deeply held moral values, creative maladjustment becomes a sane alternative to giving up altogether. Creative maladjustment consists of breaking social patterns that are morally reprehensible, taking conscious control of one's place in the environment, and readjusting to the world one lives in based on personal integrity and honesty—that is, it consists of learning to survive with minimal moral and personal compromise in a thoroughly compromised world and of not being afraid of planned and willed conflict, if necessary. (p. 130)

Many of us are afraid of conflict, especially in schools, where we have learned from our own experience as students and teachers, that conflict in schools is often met with punishment. The creative part in Kohl's admonishment to teachers, involves learning good strategies, knowing when to quietly do your own thing, when to openly challenge, and how to build a group of supports. Even so, there are risks, and therefore legitimate fears, involved in being a caring teacher. Kohl (1994) states:

> There are risks in becoming creatively maladjusted. You might get fired or find projects you have nurtured into existence destroyed by a threatened bureaucracy or conservative school board. You might find yourself under pressure at school and at home to stop making trouble and feel like giving in to the temptation to re-adjust and become silent. The choice of when, where, how, and whether to maladjust is both moral and strategic, and though it has social and educational consequences, it is fundamentally personal and private. (p. 152)

Teachers who do not tow the line, who question policy, and creatively maladjust to school cultures that do not value all children, are often dubbed as "troublemakers." The paradox is that often someone willing to take the risks involved in being a caring teacher in an environment in which care is seen as soft, as potentially dangerous, is considered a troublemaker. This can be confusing, especially for new teachers, who feel they are working from a place of moral integrity as they question school policies, only to be dubbed disruptive troublemakers, as somehow morally reprehensible. It is important for teachers to build up support networks inside of school and out, to help counteract these pressures.

Very often, being a caring teacher involves taking real risks. If teachers are taught in their own teacher training that this is the case, they may be better equipped to battle the fears that often accompany being a caring teacher. If teachers are going to become the risk-takers required for participating in significant school change, they must acknowledge both their real and imagined fears. If these fears aren't faced they can become paralyzing. It is very easy when we feel afraid to project attributes onto our students and onto school systems that make it seem futile to work for change. We must begin to recognize that when we assert that change is impossible, and become complacent in compromised values and practices, that we are most likely justifying our own inaction and giving into fear. Creative maladjustment, according to Kohl, is not an indication that we have given up on education—but just the opposite—an affirmation of its possibilities.

EXAMINING OUR AVERSIONS

In previous sections we looked at how teachers' fear can often be defended against by assigning the problem to students. Both Lindley's and Wiseman's accounts of fearful teachers resulted in the teacher's attributing the problem to students' selves instead of their own. In this section we look at how our feelings of aversion toward some students or groups of students are often based on similar attributions or projections. Often, rather than experiencing our fear directly, we experience a feeling of aversion toward another. These feelings, if understood and interrogated, can act as a signal that we need to examine ourselves, reflect into our own feelings, find the fears that underlie our strong, often bodily, reactions.

When we feel an aversion toward students, it is always an indication of something about us as well as something about them. We have been trained to look only at the student and leave our contribution out of the picture. The following story told by the brother of a boy who is developmentally delayed is a telling example of how the eye of the beholder may also be the mirror to his or her soul.

> Jon taught me to see others in a clearer light. He was my barometer. Jon evoked a reaction from everyone. Nobody was immune. And these reactions revealed each person's character. He was slow to develop, and behind his age group physically, verbally, and in independence. Even at five and six he had to be pushed in his stroller, and couldn't express himself in a manner that was recognized as "normal." No-one escaped reacting to him, even if only for a fleeting moment. And in that reaction each person's psyche was revealed, and nothing afterward could change the truth of that vision.
>
> I began to decide certain things based on those reactions: I wouldn't shop at certain stores, because the owners reactions to Jon were not kind or understanding. I judged adults around me in the manner in which they related to Jon. Some patronized him, although at the time I would have said they just acted stupidly, and couldn't communicate with him directly.
>
> Bill Prensky, Jon's brother

ABJECTION AND IDENTITY

Julia Kristeva, a French linguist and psychoanalyst, offers an interesting theory to account for the way we casually come to exclude and mistreat certain groups of people. Kristeva (1982) suggests the concept of abjection as one possible explanation for the way that apparently healthy individuals can participate in the many forms of group-based fear, hatred, and oppression. In abjection, Kristeva parallels the intense work of the self creating and defending the boundaries of identity with the construction of the exclusionary social code, the symbolic order of culture that assigns lesser identities to persons of various groups: the poor, ethnic minorities, women, persons considered to have disabilities, and gays and lesbians, to name a few. In abjection, the individual self casts the impurities of non-identity, the offensive identity elements (that's not me!), to the borders of the psychic structure. Socially, within the daily human operations of language and culture, this extrusion of waste is signified and enacted in expressions of loathing and disdain directed toward the Other. Lines are drawn and lesser spaces are created for the Other who seems to threaten the solidity of the individual at the ever-uncertain psychic borders as the Other who seems to violate the apparent purity and regularity of the social order.

Kristeva traces the roots of abjection as a psychological phenomenon in infancy. According to Kristeva, in her psychoanalytic developmental scheme, abjection is initiated when the infant reluctantly, yet necessarily, struggles to separate and differentiate itself from the mother. To the newborn, no line of demarcation exists between mother and self. The child mentally interjects the body and identity of the mother within the boundaries of self, creating a non-segmented unity, a total cosmology of child–mother. This apparent perfection is harshly interrupted as the developmental task of individuation requires an end to that psychic mother–child union. As Young (1990) explains, "the border of separation can be established only by expelling, rejecting the mother, which is only then distinguished from the infant itself" (pp. 144–145).

To the developing child, this first step toward individuation is experienced as a tenuous and traumatic rejection of the maternal aspect of self, a process in which the assertion of subject status requires a rupture of identity, an expulsion of the mother. Kristeva theorizes that this early act of mental bordering in service to subject identity provides the psychic precursor that supports a variety of forms of repulsion throughout the lifespan. Young (1990) parallels our disgust for the substances of bodily discharge with our disgust for rejected groups of persons.

Abjection may be viewed as a bodily predilection demonstrated in our disdain for body excretions. Our image of our physical self includes a separation of these substances from the physical form that we claim as our own. To some extent, I construct value in my physical body by asserting a distance and a difference from these expelled aspects of that body. Young (1990) contends that the fear and loathing produced within the rejection of specific groups of persons occurs in a similar manner and for analogous psychological reasons. The psychic self is constructed and bordered as the despised Other is constructed and walled off. What is rejected from the self—cast as negative and ugly and stands at odds with the self-identity—makes up the constitutive substance of the Other. In the opposition of the excluded and the included, a border of identity is fabricated, a place where the self ends and that which must be disconnected from the self sits in exile.

Through the explicit, political extension of Kristeva's theory of abjection into the cultural realm, Young theorizes a psychology of group oppression; of racism, sexism, classism, and ablism. Entire groups of Others—historically women, persons of color, the working class, the underclass, and persons with "disabilities"— are constructed as a means to bolster the identity of the psychic self Young calls this "the scaling of bodies" (1990, p. 122), the psychopolitical formulation of groups along a gradation of moral and physical value.

In relationship to care and cruelty in the classroom, Young and Kristeva's theorizing about abjection serve as a metaphor to help us understand feelings of aversion that we may at times feel toward some of our students or they toward us. These feelings may mask a less accessible fear of losing our own sense of personal identity. Our feelings of aversion may be seen as a signal that we need to look deeper into ourselves and how we make sense of our students. We may need to spend time examining both how the students we feel an aversion to are like us and how they are different. What do they provoke in us, bring to light, or threaten? In the following story, written by a teacher who cared enough to face up to his own aversions, we can see how examining one's aversions can lead into taking more moral responsibility for our actions and reactions.

Cal's Story: The Difference Between "Those Kids" and "Normal Kids"

In April of 1986, I got a job as a Teacher's Aide at an SED (Severely Emotionally Disturbed) center. It was a placement for violent and acting out kids. It was a very difficult job. By the end of the year I was exhausted, emotionally wrung dry. The summer of '87 I worked at a summer camp. . . . I loved it. The kids, instead of greeting me with a surly "F- you!" would run up to me, calling my name, and hug me. That was the difference, I was sure, between "normal" kids and "those" kids. By the end of the summer I felt much better.

The following year I knew I needed to find a place to be around "normal" kids on a regular basis. Otherwise I would come to believe that all kids were "like that." And by the end of the year, I would be just as bad off as I was at the end of the previous year. These were my thoughts at the time on the difference between "normal" and "those" kids, and my interactions with them. After a week in Advanced Theories of Behavior Disorders, I look back and see things much differently. "Those" kids, were angry, many if not all of them with good reason. And we (society) put them into more and more tightly controlled (structured) environments to force (encourage) them to be normal (not angry despite all that was wrong with their lives). Not liking to be controlled, they grew more and more angry and hated those (me) who tried to make them stop being angry. So "those" kids did not respond to my wonderful self with joy and I grew to intensely dislike being around them. I suspect that most of them knew it.

The "normal" kids, on the other hand, that I interacted with . . . for the most part had middle or upper middle income lives, complete with two adults. All of their needs and many of their wants were met. I interacted with them in environments that were fairly relaxed. Although there were some rules, and they had a great deal of freedom to express themselves. Also, one of the primary goals . . . was to have fun. In school, with "those" kids, one goal was to get the students to stop having fun (not that anyone in the school would have publicly admitted that). So of course, the "normal" kids enjoyed my wonderful self, and I enjoyed them.

This teacher's reflections which began with the admission that he had come to intensely dislike being around "those kids" is the starting place that allows him to realize his own contribution to relationships with students that have become hostile and hurtful. He begins to recognize both systemic and personal contributions to the toxic space that has grown between himself and the students in the SED program. From this place of personal responsibility and increased awareness of social and political contexts, this teacher can work toward engaging in more respectful and caring relationships with his students.

SHAPING CONTEXTS

Sibley (1995) adds a geographic component to this picture, explaining how social identity and location are linked within the physical landscape of the modern metropolitan area. Separations and borders are constructed in order to wall out the ostensible horrors of the impure and the disorderly, the different, the Other. Neighborhoods and homeowners attempt to purify their own living spaces by marking off in opposition those spaces and groups that threaten to disrupt the order and safety of the homogeneous home turf. Geographic purity is fabricated in opposition to defilement.

The convergence of devalued identities and spoiled spaces can be easily seen in the way upper-middle-class neighborhoods sprout up in suburban regions far from urban, non-white, working-class communities. These areas are called "good" neighborhoods with "good" schools while the urban areas are considered frightening, dirty, and unsafe. In an analogous way, gay and lesbian bars and clubs tend to be located far from straight bars and restaurants, tucked away in blemished spaces, hidden in neighborhoods or business areas of low visibility and repute. Likewise, persons considered mentally ill or mentally retarded have been traditionally segregated off to abnormal places such as asylums and hospitals for the private bearing of social stigma. Where a person is located, and who that person is taken to be, are often intimately linked (Goffman, 1961, 1963).

Within schools, we see this geographic othering when the location of special education programs, for instance, are in separate buildings and in the most inadequate of classrooms. In one district we know of, a districtwide mandate required the closing of all of the off-campus special education centers in order to be more "inclusive." However, the students from these schools, rather than being integrated into the regular school buildings, were placed in portables on the perimeter of the school and prohibited from entering the main school building, even to eat lunch. Lunches were pushed out to the students on carts. Very quickly the special education classes were designated by the other children in the school as the "boom-boom" classes and the students therein were called names.

When approached by the teachers concerning the inequity of this arrangement and the stigmatizing effect it had on the special education students, the administration expressed grave fears at allowing the special education students the same freedom to move around the school that the general education students took for granted. Their fears resonated with Kristeva's theory of abjection and Sibley's theory of geographic othering. The administration expressed fears of contamination, fears of losing control, fears that these students would somehow bring down the whole moral fiber of the school if they were allowed to mix in. The borders were fixed, they were geographically excluded to disowned, marginalized spaces, both in the social fabric of the school, as well as the physical spaces they were required to occupy.

In this example, we see fear of the Other translated into practice and policy, as students and teachers are deemed different, are labeled disordered and disturbed, and are pushed out of the main body of the school. Although this physical and social arrangement of separating out students who learn differently or act differently is being seriously challenged, the sad fact is that it is ingrained in our thinking and supported by our fears. Often, when districts move toward more socially just arrangements, such as closing down the special education centers, our fears and our aversions to those we construct as Other find new ways to structure abjection.

In the following story, told by a teacher in a graduate-level education class, we see the politics of exclusion as they play out in the contexts of a school. Her feelings of aversion toward an African American boy in her class are initially constructed as his problem, his defect. She begins to envision as a solution to move him to another place in the school, a place with students of "his kind." She wants to push him out of the space she and her other students occupy in the classroom, a school version of abjection for which the institutional mechanisms are readily available. However, in this story there is a turn of events that provides a mirror for her own meaning making, and help her see that what she had initially construed as his *problem* was much more a symptom of her own.

Judith's Story: Seeing Students Through Black and White Lenses

In order to best understand my perception of my new found career, I feel that I must make a few reflections of my past. I was born, raised and married in an all white, Protestant, republican, upper-middle class, WASP community. By the time my twenty-fifth birthday rolled around, I had married my father's business partner, bore three children, built a new house, had two new cars, was voted president of PTA, had season's passes to the Philadelphia Eagles, 76ers, Flyers, and the local tennis courts. I had it made!

By the time my 42nd birthday approached . . . I had asserted my independence and refused to take over any of the family businesses, now numbering 5, divorced my lover, father of my children, and drinking partner. After moving to Florida, I joined AA, went back to school at the local community college, and landed a position as a paraprofessional in a self-contained learning disabilities class. The administration at that school was very influential and supportive with helping me make the decision to take a leave of absence for 18 months to complete my (teaching) degree. My life was completely turned around . . . or so I thought.

D.J. was a large black boy, who had the largest white eyes and white teeth that I had ever seen, considering the fact that was the first time that I had allowed a black person close enough to be within my personal space. D.J. was labeled learning disabled. It didn't take long for me to be convinced that it was a missed diagnosis and definitely the wrong prescription to have placed D.J. in my class. He needed to be in a class for kids of his kind; retarded. When his father sent me a note, asking for more reading homework, I knew by the quality of the penmanship and his English skills that the apple didn't fall far from the tree. Later, in early Spring, his father called for an appointment for a conference. This only solidified my expert opinion that D.J. came from a lineage of functional illiterates. This puzzled me, as I tried to determine how D.J. obtained his immaculately kept designer duds.

He did not receive free lunch and always had change to buy snacks. His games that he brought in to share on "Fun Friday" always had all their pieces and did not display any tell tale signs of coming from the Salvation Army. Mr. D.J. was just as clean, neat, huge and impressive as his son. After we had a successful conference Mr. D.J. asked, Do you have any kids, Ma'am? From his enormous pants pockets he pulled out a mixture of crumpled up money and new football cards, each still encased in cellophane. "Here, take em all. I got plenty. Maybe some day they'll be worth some money." Immediately, I recognized the uniform. D.J.'s father was a local sports hero, who graduated from the State University and was drafted into the NFL.

What worth had I placed on knowing about my students care takers? If I had shared more about my own past, my hobbies, my interests, my loves and my fears, maybe D.J. would have shared information about his successful father. Why didn't I tumble off my teacher pedestal? Because of looking at my students through a one-way glass, I missed important facts that molded D.J. into the individual he was. There was never any mention of D.J.'s mother past his birth. Mr. D. J. had been D.J.'s sole parent and had raised his son, along with the help of his tightly knit family.

Do I have regrets today? You bet! I had a learning moment pass and did not have the insight to take an opportunity to find out more about a father and son relationship to help a young man who was not retarded, but big, clumsy, and shy. I missed an opportunity to be more than a spectator at a football game. . . . This may not have been my first value judgment call. It is the first that has come back to haunt me, time and time again. Unfortunately, it was not my last.

I hope that there will be another D.J. I need to experience again an apple that hasn't fallen far from the tree. I want the experience of sharing in the experience of a child following in his/her parents footsteps, wherever they may lead. . . . I want to trade my black and white glasses in for lenses that enhance the beauty of my kids, each with their complex, but unique hue. With these new wider and brighter glasses, I'm sure that it will be much easier for my kids to look back into my eyes and into my soul to see the love for them, that I hold in my heart.

Judith ends her story in a very different place than she was when it began. She has begun to realize that the ways she sees her students are not neutral nor objective, but deeply impacted by her social, cultural, and political history. She has begun to take responsibility for how she sees others, that involves looking at her own personal history and the contexts and events that have shaped her. In turn, she has begun to realize the importance of understanding the personal histories and contexts that have shaped her students.

UNINTENDED BEHAVIOR AND MORAL RESPONSIBILITY

How can we begin to break a deeply ingrained cycle of oppression that is based in our deepest fears and is reflected in the social landscapes of our lives? Young (1990) argues persuasively for an extension of moral philosophy into the realms of unintended behavior. She summarizes the basis of her position as follows:

> I have argued that oppression persists in our society partly through interactive habits, unconscious assumptions and stereotypes, and group-related feelings of nervousness and aversion. Group oppressions are enacted in this society not primarily in official laws and policies, but in informal, often unnoticed and unreflective speech, bodily reactions to others, conventional practices of everyday interaction and evaluation, aesthetic judgments, and the jokes, images and stereotypes pervading the mass media. (p. 148)

Education increasingly has been indicted as playing a central role in perpetuating racist, classist, sexist, and ablist tendencies that plague our country in spite of rhetoric that education is the great equalizer. Legislation and civil rights laws that have attempted to combat the heinous underpinnings of social oppression have had a limited effect in the absence of deep reflection and dialogue. Young (1990) speaks to these issues:

> The injunction to be just in such matters amounts to no more and no less than a call to bring the phenomena of practical consciousness and unconsciousness under discussion, that is to politicize them. The requirements of justice, then, concern less the making of cultural rules than providing institutional means for fostering politicized discussion, and making forums and media available for alternative cultural experiment and play.
>
> Cultural revolution that confronts and undermines the fears and aversions that structure unconscious behavior entails a revolution in the subject itself. (p. 152)

In Judith's story we see a revolution in Judith as she begins to confront her feelings of aversion towards D.J., feelings that find their way into forming plans to send D.J. to another place, away from Judith and her class—a gesture that sadly is easily accommodated in many schools that have an avenue for systematized abjection.

Young tells us that "the process of politicizing habits, feelings, and expressions of fantasy and desire that can foster cultural revolution entails a kind of social therapy" (1990, p. 153). This does not involve a one-on-one psychoanalytical encounter, but is more akin to the group-based consciousness raising popular in the women's movement in the late 1960s. Many educational theorists have suggested that this type of consciousness raising should be central to democratic education (e.g., Giroux, 1988; Giroux & McLaren, 1986; McLaren, 1989, 1991a; Weis, 1988).

Young (1990) makes a distinction between taking responsibility for unconscious and unintended behaviors and blaming. Blame often justifies punishment and reduces the possibility of honest self-reflection.

> To take account of such intuitions we can distinguish between blaming people and holding them responsible. . . . It is inappropriate to blame people for actions they are unaware of and do not intend. People and institutions nevertheless can and should be held responsible for unconscious and unintended behavior, actions, or attitudes that contribute to oppression.

Young stresses that consciousness raising can only occur when:

> those participating already understand something about how interactive dynamics and cultural imagery perpetuate oppression, and are committed to social justice enough to want to change them. Such activity cannot take place in the abstract. People will be motivated to reflect on themselves and their relations with others only in concrete social circumstances where they recognize problems. (p. 155)

In agreement with Young, it is our position that in order to bring a transformation in educational structures, practices, and policies in such a way as to create more just environments, educators need to be involved in a critical reflective process of raising issues of social oppression to consciousness. Teacher education is positioned as the likely place for such critical reflection to occur. Educational research and practice, as it is being revised by critical theorists (Giroux, 1991, 1988; Kincheloe, 1991; McLaren, 1989, 1991b, 1994), feminist theorists (Hernandez, 1997; Kelly, 1997; Luke, 1992), and cultural theorists (Delpit, 1993; Foster, 1994; Greene, 1997), provide avenues of support and various narrative and interpretive methodologies for this therapeutic and transformative process.

PRACTICES AND PROCESSES THAT
FOSTER CRITICAL SELF-REFLECTION

In a sense, critical self-reflection is the process that allows for the alchemy of cruel practices into caring practices. It is a process that can move us from a place of unknowing to knowing in relationship to our contributions to the space between ourselves and our students. This can be seen in the critical stories told by Cal and Judith in this chapter. In both cases, these teachers were able to reflect on situations with students in which their own actions, interactions, and ways of seeing and making sense of their students were limited by their own fear, prejudice, and feelings of aversion. Their willingness to face these less-desirable aspects of their teacher selves is an act of caring. They were willing to face the painful recognition of the cruel teacher in themselves. This was a door to change. In each story we see a transformed consciousness and a renewed commitment to working with students in more caring ways. In both cases, these teachers made a conscious decision to take responsibility for the way they *see* students, recognizing that their seeing was as much a part of who they were as who their students were. This is the essence of an emerging critical consciousness.

Both Cal and Judith were students in a class taught by the first author (Smith) when they wrote these critical stories of self. They were involved in a graduate-level class that focused on critical self-reflection. One of the texts for the course was Smith's autobiography in which she critically examines her own teaching experiences. This text does not present Smith as the perfect teacher, but one who increasingly realizes that teaching is a very complex and difficult job in which one is always learning about oneself, one's students, systems, power, and culture. Many of the students openly discussed how important it was for them to have these stories of their professor's teaching experiences which were full of human unknowing as well as knowing. It gave them space to look into their own selves without feeling they would be judged.

When we admit to our students our own fears and vulnerabilities, as well as our joys and convictions, we give them room to move into these spaces without the fear of judgment. This is no less true at the university level than it is at grade school level. Teacher education that is deeply grounded in authentic relationships in which the professor is vulnerable, fallible, and knowable helps create a space for teachers and preservice teachers to explore aspects of their own experiences and beliefs that may contribute to cruel practices. This examination often is the key to transformation.

Conversely, teacher education classes that hold to unspoken assumptions that teachers should be perfect human beings, completely selfless and free of prejudice, contribute to the socialization of educators who secretly fear that they are unworthy to be teachers. This fear, which has been addressed previously in this chapter, can easily become the source of cruelty if it is unexamined. In like manner, texts that do not examine the complexity of teaching, and ignore the complex relationships among human beings, contribute to cruel practices because they do not provide teachers with experiences, examples, or processes that would help them critically examine their teaching practices.

CRITICAL STORIES OF SELF

Danforth (the second author) has written a series of critical stories of self that story the perilous journey into his own racist, classist, sexist, and ablist behaviors. These stories include incidents from his life that reflect his own cruel actions or inactions, as well as the contexts of his life that helped shape and support this cruelty. In one story, called "Peanut Butter and Jelly," Danforth (1997) recounts an incident from his elementary school days when a group of children assaulted a local boy and his sister in a ritual of humiliation. Their crime, it seems, was their lack of material resources, their poor, working-class status evidenced especially to Danforth by the $3.98 pair of tennis shoes worn by the boy. Danforth, under the extreme social pressure of elementary school culture and in congruence with his own family's strong Protestant work ethic (which avowed that anyone who worked hard enough could prosper, and conversely, anyone who didn't prosper did not work hard enough and was, therefore, somewhat morally inferior), participated, albeit ambivalently, in the vicious acts continuously heaped upon these children.

Judith's and Cal's stories in this chapter were written as an assignment that was given in conjunction with reading Danforth's critical stories. Stories like Danforth's provide educators and future educators with an example of critical reflective thinking that gives new depth and meaning to the rhetoric of reflective teaching in the literature. On a personal level, Judith and Cal have been changed by their writing. The type of hermeneutic learning that came from critically looking into their pasts will inevitably change who they are in the future. As these teachers construct stories of unintentionally devaluing others in their pasts, they also look to the future with clear intentions. Judith wants to change her glasses which have caused her to see children in terms of black and white and Cal will never again be able to see "those" students as separate from the oppressive school environments or his attitudes toward them.

Beyond the personal learning and transformation, these teachers' stories open up a space for other teachers to begin to look into their own disowned pasts. They open up a space for dialogue among educators that is personal, social, political, and critical. Cal and Judith shared their stories in class, as did many of the other class members. Each person benefited from the others' honesty and insights. Each story allowed the students to reflect on, gave them room to examine in a group, their own lenses and practices. This allowed for a deep personal learning and a growing social consciousness of the less visible dynamics involved in being a caring teacher. The assumption that we just need to learn the right methods and teach the right curriculum has obscured the extremely perplexing moral issues involved in education. The belief that we can be neutral and objective has worked against the kinds of critical reflection that could bring significant social and political change.

OPENING UP CLASSROOM SPACES FOR DIALOGUE

The letter-writing process that has served as a data source for this text has resulted in hundreds of letters written to teachers perceived as caring and cruel. One wonders how many of the teachers who were focused on in the letters about classroom cruelty had any idea that their students felt damaged by their actions. Teachers rarely speak about or acknowledge the ways they may hurt their students. One wonders if they know the pain they have caused since students rarely feel safe challenging their teacher's actions. When students do question classroom practices, they are often perceived as defiant, and rather than being heard, they are silenced, punished, or shamed.

One of the first conscious steps one can take to becoming a more caring teacher is by providing avenues for students to express their feelings in the class about their own treatment, perceptions, joys, and hurts. This should happen in informal ways, where teachers ask for their students' opinions, advice, and feedback naturally in the course of the day. And it should happen in more structured ways where students are asked to respond periodically to questionnaires, surveys, and classroom inventories that address classroom atmosphere and teacher–student relationships. A very good collection of these kinds of surveys can be found in Jones and Jones (1998) *Comprehensive Classroom Management.* One questionnaire given to students by the teacher involve such questions as:

- Am I courteous toward you?
- Am I honest?
- Do I smile at you?
- Can you ask questions in class?

In this particular questionnaire, students can rate the teacher from one to five. Similar questionnaires are designed to be sent to families of students asking for their feedback.

One of the most important, yet least utilized, forms of feedback come when students are angry or complaining in class. When a student lashes out at a teacher in anger, it is often a result of feeling hurt or discounted. Too often, teachers respond with more pressure or punishment which only deepens the hurt and the surface anger. Kohl, in his essay "I Won't Learn From You," (1994) tells a wonderful story of what is possible when teachers listen to their students' criticisms. Kohl describes an African American student named Akmir who quietly and fiercely challenged Freudian psychology as a "white man's theory," and when Kohl asked him to explain, responded that there was no point in trying to explain it to a white man. Kohl responded that he was wrong about that in this case and invited him to join the class and encouraged his comments. Kohl tells the story:

> Akmir read everything, studied it thoroughly, and came to class prepared to argue. He read all the material aggressively, looking for sentences or phrases that indicated or could be interpreted to imply racism, ranging from uses of words "black" and "dark" to signify evil to sophisticated arguments that implied the superiority of Western culture. For a few sessions the class was dominated by his questioning of our texts. At first I thought it was a game meant to provoke me, but it soon became clear that that was an egotistic response on my part. . . . I learned from Akmir's analyses how I fell into sloppy, racist linguistic habits and came to take his criticisms seriously. I tried to read texts from his point of view and pick out the phrases and

thoughts that he might find offensive. In some cases, it made reading familiar material very uncomfortable. (pp. 18–19)

In Kohl's account we see what is possible when we get beyond feeling like every conflict is a personal affront. The kind of learning that we can engage in when we listen to our students takes us beyond our own way of seeing and allows us to see with them. This cannot happen if we do not allow students to speak their minds and their hearts in our classes. In order to do this we must push beyond our fear of the live encounter with others who do not share our histories, cultures, perspectives or position within the school.

A stunning account of the kind of learning that can occur when we learn to listen to each other and not discount others' views can be seen in the documentary film *The Color of Fear* (Wah, 1994). In this film, we see a dialogue among a group of men of diverse cultural and ethnic heritages. The group is made up of three Asian, two Hispanic, two African American, and two European American men. There are times when the participants express anger and outrage, especially at the one European American man who continuously tells them their views are unfounded. But the dialogue persists and deep personal learning occurs as the men begin to listen to each other with their hearts. Classrooms provide the opportunity for deep personal learning as well, for students and teachers, but we have to make them safe places to disagree, and even to express anger. Anger, rather than being punished, should be seen as a signal that very important personal learning can occur if we as teachers don't shut down the dialogue.

One wonders what would have happened if the letters written to teachers in our study had been written at the time students were experiencing the care and cruelty they attest to. What would happen if we invited our students to write letters to us telling us about the times we helped them the most and the times we hurt them the most, when we still had time to help heal the wounds, change our practices, and reflect on our relationships?

CONSCIOUSLY COMMITTING TO CARE

We have tried to make visible the dimensions of schooling that have been hidden and to tell stories that have been censored. These are stories about the profound influence our relationships within educational contexts have on our sense of self and other. In stories of teachers who have helped us we see the great potential educators have to impact students' lives and identities in significant ways. In examining teachers' stories about their experiences in schools we see that students have great potential to impact educators' lives and identities as well. These stories warm us and inspire us to be caring teachers. Few people go into this profession with the intention to harm the children in their care. And yet the stories of hurt and cruelty suffered at the hands of teachers and within the walls of schools resonates too clearly. If we are to create schools that embrace all children, we must delve beyond the surface of our good intentions to unearth the often unrecognized fears and aversions that all too often become unintended cruelty.

The deep-seated capacity of human beings to cast others into a group of less worth, and then to apply different rules to their care, has been played out over and over in human history with such viciousness as to make us both ashamed and afraid. When viewed from a distance of time and space, atrocities like the Holocaust make us tremble, and we somehow convince ourselves that those who participated in these crimes were a different sort of human being than us. However, in this act of separating ourselves out as different and superior we follow the same recipe which led to those atrocities, though on a smaller scale.

It is our hope that this book will help teachers and prospective teachers to think deeply about the relational spaces they share with students and to consciously commit to working toward being more caring teachers. This involves more than simply good intentions or even good feelings toward our students. It entails making a conscious commitment to keeping the space between students and ourselves open for dialogue, reflection, and change. This may well begin with an activity like writing letters to our teachers that we do not intend to send. It may extend beyond that to a more systematic examination of our own schooling and personal history. It may involve writing critical stories of self, examining our own histories for racist, sexist, classist, or ablist beliefs which may contaminate our relationships with students in unintended ways. Once we have entered that space through memory, imagination, writing, and dialogue, we can look more deeply at our relationships with our own students or future students.

Examining the relational space between students and teachers means many things. It means examining our curriculum and classroom structures for the impact they have on students' sense of identity. Caring involves actively trying to see and hear and feel from our students' perspectives. It means allowing ourselves to be vulnerable, taking chances and risks, looking at our own fears, and interrogating our aversions. It means reflecting on our practices, both in solitude and with our students. Caring involves learning about our students' cultures and histories, spending time in their neighborhoods, reading literature, and viewing art that will help us embrace them and cherish them, rather than fear them.

Caring means we are willing to face up to and explore the instances when we are hurtful to students, examining our cultural lenses, questioning our beliefs and values. Caring means setting up democratic classrooms where students feel free to speak their hearts as well as their minds. Caring means taking time to develop a mode of ethical decision making, continuously learning to improve our practices, and taking to heart the incredible responsibility that teaching entails.

Caring for our students ultimately begins in caring for ourselves, facing our own hurts in schools in the past as students and in the present as teachers. It means working to heal and repair our own alienation within schools through developing support groups and friendships. Caring for ourselves means giving ourselves room to be human, to make mistakes, to have limitations, and to be afraid. It also means taking responsibility for our failures, limitations, and biases and continuously working toward deeper understanding of ourselves, as well as our students and systems.

Teaching is very difficult work that can never be adequately measured by gains in reading levels or scores on standardized tests. We need to acknowledge the less visible, but profoundly important, relational aspects of teaching, and make a conscious decision to color those spaces with care. This is not something we can do alone, or once and for all, but is an endeavor with which we need our students to continuously help us. And in that need, we open ourselves to learn from our students and honor them as teachers as well as learners. In this reciprocal and mutual learning we engage in the most important pedagogy of all: the lifelong quest of learning to be more human and more humane. This is the priceless opportunity that classrooms offer. Care is what moves us beyond our fears to embrace the incredible potential that is there.

REFERENCES

Danforth, S. (1997). Autobiography as critical pedagogy: Locating myself in class-based oppression. *Teaching Education, 9*(1), 3–14.

Delpit, L. D. (1993). The silenced dialogue: Power and pedagogy in educating other people's children. In L. Weis & M. Fine (Eds.), *Beyond silenced voices: Class, race, and gender in United States schools.* Albany: State University of New York Press.

Foster, M. (1994). The power to one thing is never the power to know all things: Methodological notes on two studies of black American teachers. In A. Gitlin (Ed.), *Power and method: Political activism and educational research.* New York: Routledge.

Giroux, H. A. (1988). *Teachers as intellectuals: Toward a critical pedagogy of learning.* New York: Bergin & Garvey.

Giroux, H. A. (1991). Postmodernism as border pedagogy: Redefining the boundaries of race and ethnicity. In H. A. Giroux (Ed.) *Postmodernism, feminism, and cultural politics: Redrawing educational boundaries* (pp. 217–256). Albany: State University of New York Press.

Giroux, H. A., & McLaren, P. (1986). Teacher education and the politics of engagement: The case for democratic schooling. *Harvard Educational Review, 56*(3), 213–238.

Goffman, E. (1961). Asylums: Essays on the social situation of mental patients and other inmates. Garden City, NY: Anchor Books.

Goffman, E. (1963). Stigma: Notes on the management of spoiled identity. Englewood Cliffs, NJ: Prentice-Hall.

Greene, M. (1997). Exclusions and awakenings. In A. Neumann & P. L. Peterson (Eds.), *Learning from our lives: Women, research, and autobiography in education* (pp. 18–36). New York: Teachers College Press.

Hernandez, A. (1997). *Pedagogy, democracy and feminism: Rethinking the public sphere.* Albany: State University of New York Press.

Jones, V., & Jones, L. (1998). *Comprehensive classroom management: Creating communities of support and solving problems* (5th ed.). Boston: Allyn and Bacon.

Kelly, U. A. (1997). *Schooling desire: Literacy, cultural politics, and pedagogy.* New York: Routledge.

Kincheloe, J. (1991). *Teachers as researchers: Qualitative inquiry as a path to empowerment.* Bristol, PA: Falmer Press.

Kohl, H. (1994). *I won't learn from you and other thoughts on creative maladjustment.* New York: New Press.

Kristeva, J. (1982). Powers of horror: An essay in abjection. New York: Columbia University Press.

Lindley, D. A. (1993). *This rough magic: The life of teaching.* Westport, CT: Bergin & Garvey.

Luke, C. (1992). Feminist politics in radical pedagogy. In C. Luke and J. Gore (Eds.), *Feminisms and critical pedagogy.* New York: Routledge.

McLaren, P. (1989). Life in schools: An introduction to critical pedagogy in the foundations of education. New York: Longman.

McLaren, P. (1991a). Critical pedagogy: Constructing an arch of social dreaming and a doorway to hope. *Journal of Education, 173*(1), 9–34.

McLaren, P. (1991b). Schooling the postmodern body: Critical pedagogy and the politics of enfleshment. In H. A. Giroux (Ed.), *Postmodernism, feminism, and cultural politics: Redrawing educational boundaries* (pp. 144–173). Albany: State University of New York Press.

McLaren, P. (1994). Multiculturalism and the postmodern critique: Toward a pedagogy of resistance and transformation. In H. A. Giroux & P. McLaren (Eds.), *Between borders: Pedagogy and the politics of cultural studies* (pp. 192–219). New York: Routledge.

Miller, A. (1990). *Thou shalt not be aware: Society's betrayal of the child.* New York: Meridian.

Palmer, P. (1998). *The courage to teach: Exploring the inner landscape of a teacher's life.* San Francisco: Jossey-Bass.

Sibley, D. (1995). *Geographies of exclusion: Society and difference in the West.* Lincoln: University of Nebraska Press.

Weis, L. (Ed.). (1988). Class, race, and gender in American education. Albany, NY: State University of New York Press.

Wah, L. M. (Producer), & Hunter, M. (Director). (1994). *The color of fear* [Film]. Oakland, CA: Stir-Fry Productions.

Wiseman, A. (1993). *Crackpot: A Novel.* Lincoln: University of Nebraska Press.

Young, I. M. (1990). Justice and the politics of difference. Princeton, NJ: Princeton University Press.

Author Index

Subject Index